GOD, COUNTRY, NOTRE DAME...AND LACROSSE

NOTRE DAME CLUB LACROSSE MILITARY VETERANS IN THEIR OWN WORDS

EDITED BY

LEN NIESSEN, JERRY KAMMER, DAVE JURUSIK

D0813415

ISBN 978-1-6671-7789-2

Photo credits: Color lacrosse portraits: Pete Sillari. Black and white lacrosse portraits: Jack Tate. Dedication page team photo: Len Niessen. All other photos provided by the essayists unless credited with photo

Cover photos: Lacrosse Player on Rockne Memorial Building (Len Niessen)

God Country Notre Dame Portal, Sacred Heart Basilica, Notre Dame (internet)

Back Cover: ND Blanket w Sword and Lacrosse Stick (Tom Moran). The stick pictured scored the first goal in ND lacrosse history

To the Notre Dame Club Lacrosse Brotherhood

"I don't believe an accident of birth makes people sisters or brothers. It makes them siblings, gives them mutuality of parentage. Sisterhood and brotherhood is a condition people have to work at." – Maya Angelou

Contents

Preface

The inspiration for this tribute to the veterans among the members of the Notre Dame lacrosse brotherhood came from an email chain started on Veteran's Day, 2020. Dave Jurusik '73 thought that those emails would make a great story. And what better way to tell that story than to have it in the vets' own words. We asked the vets to tell us how they chose Notre Dame, what they recall most vividly about the lacrosse team and where their military service took them, and what they did post military. We wanted to know their stories.

The stories have been grouped into three eras of ND lacrosse players: Those who graduated between 1964 and 1968, during the Wooden Stick Era; those who graduated between 1969 and 1974 in The Hybrid Stick Era; and those who graduated between 1975 and the beginning of varsity lacrosse in 1981, during the Plastic Head Era. Interestingly, those periods reflect in US Military involvement as well: the intensification of the Vietnam War, the protracted winding down of the war and the post-war period.

We also wanted to honor those in the brotherhood that served their country in the Peace Corps. Those stories are included as well.

Also included here are stories about our veteran brothers that are deceased; those stories are told by their teammates and family members.

Finally, no story about Notre Dame lacrosse can be told without mentioning two key individuals: Jack Tate and Rich O'Leary. Though they didn't serve in the military, their stories are included here, told by men close to them.

Thanks to all of the veterans for their service and also for their participation in this project.

Thanks also to Claire Gray for her comprehensive proofreading of our manuscript.

TD Paulius provided access to his portraits and also legal advice.

Much gratitude goes to my co-editors, Jerry and Dave for their many hours spent on this project and their response to my many, many emails.

Credit must also be given to John Corcoran '75 whose email to me on November 11, 2020 got the email ball rolling.

-Len Niessen April 2021

Introduction

I am particularly honored to write an introduction to this compilation of the experiences of Notre Dame lacrosse team members who are also Veterans. This is a singular honor not just because of the large number of men who lived both experiences, and not just because of the debt we all owe to these Vets, but most importantly because of the shared values that run through Notre Dame, military service, and the lacrosse program.

The intersections of the fundamental personal beliefs that Notre Dame and ND Lacrosse teach everyday with the fundamentals of duty and honor that are the foundation of service are many and varied. These mutual traits are best recalled through the experiences of those that lived them, and best told with the insight, reverence and humor that each story seems to include.

Thank you to those who contributed their stories, thank you to those who shared these experiences and brought the color to the stories, and thank you to all who have served our country and our University.

Kevin Corrigan, Baumer Family Head Coach, Notre Dame Lacrosse

Chapter 1

The Wooden Stick Era '64-'68

E veryone knows about the '60s. It was a time of great change, social unrest, riots, assassinations, landmark civil rights legislation and a foreign undeclared war that, as the decade moved toward its end, came more and more to the foreground, especially for college age men. At Notre Dame, we students reacted to all of those events but probably not to the same extent that Cal Berkeley or some of the more liberal colleges in the Northeast did. We had protests and marches for Medgar Evers and Dow Chemical recruiters, but we also had three branches of ROTC on campus. On a typical day on campus you would see students with beards dressed in old Army jackets walking to class alongside cadets in uniform. And no matter how we felt about the war in Vietnam, we mostly got along with each other. After all, we were roommates and teammates.

Every lacrosse player from this era faced the reality of Vietnam. Many graduated and immediately became members of the military which almost always meant Vietnam. Several went into the Peace Corps and several took advantage of deferments, first student and then occupational. The Draft Lottery came later, so those not in ROTC faced the specter of The Draft.

Lacrosse was born in 1964, the brainchild of Monogram Fencer Jack Tate. Jack was a true visionary but also a guy that could get things done and inspire others at the same time. The ND Lacrosse Club was never short of players but at the beginning, it was very short on experience. There were a handful of men that had prior lacrosse experience but there were athletes from other high school sports throughout the roster. And there was a general philosophy that if we can't "out finesse" them, we could "out condition" and "out work" them. We refer to the pioneers from the 1964 squad as "The First Team" and many of their stories appear on these pages.

The equipment we used would look in place in a museum of ancient history. In fact, I have my wooden attack stick mounted on the wall in our family room, and I'm not the only one that does. Our helmets were mis-matched, some white leather, some brown leather. I remember playing against Michigan State and one of their players wore a green football helmet. Our gloves were a mixture of lacrosse and hockey gloves. Many of our players took advantage of the used football spikes offered by the athletic department, and I was one of those players.

The wooden sticks require more discussion. There were no two sticks that were exactly alike. Some heads were curved at the top but most were flat. Some shafts were straight as an arrow, others not so much. I had a stick that had a knot in the shaft that left a divot. The heads were a combination of leather and gut that did not fare well in rainy weather. We used the tongue depressors from the first aid kit to try to keep the gut wall from curling up. When the sticks broke, we tried to fix them with bandage and fiberglass. A fiberglassed stick, heavy to begin with, became a real weapon. The heads were larger than today's sticks which was probably a good thing for us lacrosse novices.

We had no coach. The guys on that first team in 1964 had a faculty advisor, Professor Harry Saxe (rhymes with Lax), who had played college lacrosse at CCNY but he was strictly in the background. Our coaching came from our captains, Jack Tate, Jim Salscheider, Bill Joseph, and Matt Dwyer along with the few other players that had prior lacrosse experience. I still find it astounding that we managed to win as many games as we did during this era, and we beat both club and varsity programs.

We managed to have a lot of fun. Ask the players from this era about their lacrosse experience and you are likely to first hear about the road trips, the parties and various escapades. And for sure, you will hear about friends made for life.

Jack Tate '64

Jack Tate was the man that started the Notre Dame lacrosse program in 1964. He died in 2010 but not before he saw his creation rise to the highest level of collegiate lacrosse. This remembrance was written by Len Niessen.

The Founder of Notre Dame Lacrosse

Most of the men who played lacrosse at Notre Dame between 1964 and 1980 know this Creation Story. About how Jack "Boomer" Tate, from Allentown, PA who had played every sport but lacrosse, brought lacrosse to Notre Dame. According to Jack, (this is the story he swore to) after a shoulder injury put him out of action for football, he tried fencing. There, Jack earned an ND monogram, but somehow it wasn't enough. Then one day while lying on his bed off-campus, a "vision" came to Jack calling him to bring lacrosse to Notre Dame du Lac. And this is exactly what he did, even though he had never played or even seen the game played before. With a creation story like that, probably apocryphal and definitely mythical, the Notre Dame Lacrosse Program must have been destined for greatness!

Even before a team was fielded, Jack petitioned for and obtained a charter for lacrosse as a club sport. After consulting with Jim Adams, the lacrosse coach at Army and Bob Scott of Johns Hopkins, Jack had enough knowledge to start to recruit a team, which turned out to be an easy task. By placing flyers in each dorm to announce a team meeting, he rounded up over one hundred prospective players, eighty of whom would remain on the team. With the help of legends Moose Krause and Nappy Napolitano, the team was able to secure the necessary equipment to play a season of eleven games. The schedule, which was finalized long before a team had been assembled, included a tournament hosted by the team and a road trip over the Easter break. Jack not only had a vision, but he was also able to get others to buy in and help make it happen. The team ended up 5-6, not bad considering their opponents had been playing lacrosse for years.

The men who played on the first Irish lacrosse team have strong opinions about Jack. Dan Manion '64 said, "Jack Tate was a true leader. He embodied a lot of the qualities that Notre Dame was all about." Jim Salscheider '65 called Jack "the greatest leader I've met in my lifetime." Rick "Zeke" Sheahan '65 said "Jack made all the difference in my life." Pete Sillari '66 said simply "I love Jack Tate".

Pete Ricchiuti '64 summed it up, "How Jack created a team from nothing in less than a year, got us gear, a full schedule, an Easter trip, an invitational tournament and everything else defies belief."

In keeping with his vision, that this was not some rag tag organization, Jack took every First Team member's photo, in uniform, with the Golden Dome in the background and gave each a copy.

Around 1999, I sent Jack a copy of an essay I had written about my years on the team in the mid '60's. Jack called me at work (I have no idea how he got my number) and gave me my marching orders: yeah, the essay was great but here's what you need to do.... Expand the essay to include all the club years from 1964 to 1980, turn it into a book, send a copy to the ND library, a copy to the Lacrosse Hall of Fame and have the ND Bookstore sell the book. That phone call led to "The Golden Years, A History of Club Lacrosse at Notre Dame." There is a copy in general circulation at the Hesburgh library, in the ND Archives, at the Lacrosse Hall of Fame, and yes, for a time it was available at the ND Bookstore... just as Jack had envisioned.

Jack returned to ND as a graduate student to help run things (probably for an education too). As if creating the program in 1964 were not enough, he felt there was more work to be done. So in 1966, Jack created the Lacrosse Alumni Association in order to keep the grads engaged with the team. Out of this came an alumni game in 1967 where Notre Dame Lacrosse Alumni scrimmaged the undergraduates, a tradition that endured for many years.

Jack received his master's degree from Notre Dame in 1966 and worked on Wall Street for many years. He passed away in 2010 at the age of 67, leaving his wife Michele and daughter Stacey. Before he died Jack was able to see his creation, Notre Dame Lacrosse, play against Duke in the National Championship game in Baltimore... probably just as he had envisioned!

Jim Dixon '64

Jim Dixon came to Notre Dame from Syracuse, NY and was a midfielder and member of the first Irish lacrosse team in 1964. An Army ROTC member, he graduated with a BS in Mechanical Engineering and served in Korea in the Engineering Corps. Jim's post Army career was in engineering.

Engineering Grad Serves with Army in Korea

The year was 1964. A guy named Jack Tate was recruiting across campus for the new ND Lacrosse Club's initial season. I met the minimum requirement, no experience. My previous exposure to lacrosse growing up outside of Syracuse, NY was seeing box lacrosse fields on Indian reservations across Central New York (high school lacrosse was still years away in the area) and hearing stories that the early Indian game was played cross-country between tribes, the ball could be carried in your mouth, you had a weapon (a stick), and could draw a penalty only if you drew blood. The term "fact checking" wasn't in the lexicon at the time but the story sounded pretty cool.

What do I remember about ND lacrosse? The stadium steps. Boomer told us that we would be less experienced than many of the teams we would play against but that we would develop stamina that would turn the tide late in games, and it paid off; it helped us go 5 and 6 that first season. (We did have some great, experienced players like Jim Salscheider, Tom Moran, and Cliff "the Stork" Lennon.) I was far from a star. As a third-string scrub I got into just one late season home game in the 2nd Half. I won one ground ball (yes, I scooped through it) and had one shot, almost-on-goal (it went just over the crossbar) but I still remember those two plays like it was yesterday. I was a senior in '64 and played just that one season but the ND Lacrosse camaraderie, teamwork, and work ethic have helped shape the rest of my life.

I was Army ROTC and, with a BSME, went into the Army Engineers. It was '66, early in the Vietnam buildup and I volunteered for Nam; so, they sent me to Korea. Friends ribbed me about applying reverse psychology but that wasn't so. Actually, the Army was being logical; the experienced engineering officers were being sent to Nam and us young greenhorns were being sent to places like Korea to backfill the resulting openings.

I was first assigned to a Corp of Engineers facility at Munsan Eup, one mile from the DMZ, where the key memory was hearing the North Korean propaganda broadcast by loud speakers across the DMZ every night.

The most memorable experience of my tour-of-duty in Korea came when I was a new 2nd Lieutenant and had just been assigned as a Company Commander of the Equipment and Maintenance Company of the 802 Construction Engineering Division in Pyeongtaek, 65 km south of Seoul on the Yellow Sea. The company had 200+ US enlisted, 243 Korean enlisted augmentation troops and 40+ Korean heavy equipment mechanics. We ran a rock quarry with a WWII era rock crusher, had a World War II vintage asphalt plant and heavy equipment like 40 Ton cranes as well as a fleet of dump trucks, bulldozers, road graders, etc. If it sounds more like a civilian construction company than a military unit that's because it was, and we worked like one too, doing construction eight to twelve hours a day.

A major problem was that over half of the equipment was parked on the "deadline" needing repair, and not available for work. A second problem was that we had a responsibility to train the Korean troops to operate the trucks and equipment but they were only being used for pick and shovel work. The key to improvement was depending on the experience and advice of my Top Sergeant and the other experienced NCOs and, after agreeing on goals, giving them the latitude to plan and execute their part.

Our Supply Sergeant was resourceful (aren't they all). He would go to the big Army depot in Pusan with a few soldiers and crawl around the dusty attics of old depot buildings, identifying parts for old equipment that was out-of-production and not available through regular requisitioning. A few days later he would call and tell us how many flatbeds to send to pick up all the stuff he found. Of course, we had to send some items that he needed to horse trade for the things we were getting.

On the training front, we assigned one US soldier driver and one Korean trainee to each truck and piece of equipment. In the dump trucks, the partners bonded, shared the driving, and, at the end of the day, after 8+ hours on a construction job, they would wash "their truck" before parking it in the motor pool. They would inspect their equipment every day and put in a maintenance request for any leak or other work that was needed. Our equipment availability went up by more than 90%, we completed many projects that helped the Koreans rebuild their country, and we won the Best Engineering Unit in Korea award in competition with 40 other companies.

As it might show, I am enthusiastic about that great experience, and it again reinforced the belief that in drawing on the knowledge of your folks and building teamwork to overcome obstacles a lot can be accomplished.

Post military, I enjoyed a rewarding career in engineering and management in manufacturing companies. Just to give one example, in the 1980s I had an electronics manufacturing plant in El Salvador reporting to me; this was during its civil war. We had the only US owned factory; all of the other US companies had moved their operations elsewhere. El Salvador had an election coming up and the rebels were burning buses so the government couldn't transport voters to the polls. One morning, the rebels stopped a bus carrying workers to our plant, ushered them off the bus and burned the bus. You might think the ladies would turn around and go home, but no, they walked the remaining seven miles to the plant to work. Talk about being motivated to help working people improve their lives.

I retired at 65 and then taught high school math for ten years in the small farming community of Immokalee, FL where the poverty rate is 44%. Helping those young people succeed was *muy gratificante*. As an aside, four of the "kids" who graduated while I was there are now in the NFL. (Unfortunately, ND recruiters weren't successful.) Ultimately, the ND and ND Lacrosse experience helped shape my approach to challenges (opportunities) throughout my career. Go Irish!

Jim Dixon c1966   *Jim Dixon and Len Niessen 2015*

Mike Luea '64

Mike Luea came to Notre Dame from Flint, Michigan in 1960. He was a midfielder on the first Notre Dame lacrosse team in 1964 and also reported on the team in the student newspaper, The Voice. Mike graduated in 1964 with a BS in Chemistry and Biology and spent the next two years in the Peace Corps. He got his master's in Social Work from University of Michigan. Mike worked for Michigan Family Independence as a social worker. He lives in Lansing, Michigan with his wife Barbara.

First Teamer Overcomes Injury, Serves in Peace Corps

"We know that all things work for good for those who love God, who are called according to His purpose" (Romans 8:28)

I attended a Catholic High School for four years and in my senior year the assistant parish priest wanted me to go to the seminary and study to be a priest. I felt a lot of pressure from him. I said a prayer that the Good Lord would show me which path to take. A recruiter from ND came to our school and made a presentation on what the college was like. I applied and was accepted. I figured that was my "sign" to skip the priesthood! ND was the only college I applied to. My grandfather had set aside money for each of the six kids in my family to go to college, so the "price was right"!

In my last year at Notre Dame, I experienced a shock that would change my life. At lacrosse practice on October 23,

1963, I was smacked in the right eye by a teammate's lacrosse stick that poked through my facemask. The blow gave me a shiner and then I started having severe headaches. The university doctor determined I had hemorrhaging in the eye and I should return to my hometown of Flint and see a specialist. Thus began an unchosen odyssey, a long road of discovery of who I am and what I am here for.

Before the accident I expected to earn a BS degree in Pre-Med, find a medical school, and enjoy a comfortable life as a physician. At a hospital in Flint, as I confronted the severity of my injury, I had to face my worst fear. I could lose my eye, be required to repeat senior year, and because my grades were just average, I risked not being accepted at a med school. As I lay in a hospital bed late at night, my eye covered with a compression bandage, and my whole future a blur, I prayed and talked to God with both fear and a sort of wry fatalism: "Go ahead, do whatever you want with my life." With visions of magazine ads that featured a man wearing an eye patch, I said, "Just don't make me a Hathaway shirt salesman." An unexpected peace immediately came over me immediately. It was as if God heard me, and everything was going to be OK.

My worst fears were partially relieved when the surgeon told me that the eye would not have to be removed. But there would be permanent damage to the retina, and I would have only peripheral vision in my dominant eye. It seemed that I had to resign myself to the fact that I'd never be a doctor with only one eye functioning.

In January 1964 I returned to Notre Dame, knowing I needed

to play lacrosse again and face the fear of getting hit again by somebody's stick. As a second teamer I experienced the ups and downs of an almost-winning season with my teammates.

In March a teammate, John Turner approached me after practice and asked me, "Mike, how about if we go down to the Post Office and apply for this new program called the Peace Corps?" I always respected John and his ideas. And though I knew nothing about the Peace Corps, I applied.

Within two months I received a letter from Washington saying the Peace Corps had accepted me for work in Ecuador.

My two years in the Peace Corps were some of the best times of my life. After four months training in Missouri and Puerto Rico I was off to Ecuador, where I was assigned to work in a "squatters" neighborhood in the hot, steamy port city of Guayaquil. I set up a medical clinic primarily for women and children. One major goal was to reduce the infant mortality rate, which at the time was extremely high.

Part of the plan was for me to move into the neighborhood. I rented a stucco house that sat on stilts two blocks from the house that we would convert into a clinic. This was a neighborhood perched on the edge of a tidal flat area. During the rainy season water would surround all our houses and flood underneath our floors. A single dirt road connected our main street to where the bus would stop to take people out to the city's established neighborhoods. We had electricity but no running water.

What made the time in Ecuador so meaningful was the people I lived and worked with. It took us almost three months to get our clinic up and running. You could see the hope and pride in the neighbors in helping prepare the rental property to be "their clinic". In the evenings, we would sit around and talk on the cement steps of the local "*tienda*" until late evening. We shared stories, sipped an occasional beer, and shared Kool cigarettes. As I worked with these new friends for 20 months, I learned how to appreciate their contentment about life, their families, their manual labor jobs, and their hopes and dreams. I was honored to be asked to be the *padrino* (godfather) for 13 of their children.

At the end of my two-year tour, when I was asked what I had accomplished, I said: "We probably treated over 4,300 women and children at our clinic. We probably extended the life of the majority of those babies and children. As a result, Ecuador has at least five more teachers, 20 more lawyers, a handful of new medical personnel and others who otherwise would have not made it." I strongly believe, we made a difference!

Near the end of my Peace Corps tour of duty, I found out that the University of Michigan had a special graduate program in the School of Social Work for returned Peace Corps volunteers. It would lead to a Master's Degree in Social Work. It was just what I wanted. My first job for 1 ½ years was with the State of Michigan, as the primary worker to assist county welfare offices to serve the 27,000 migrant workers and their families who came to Michigan to help harvest the vegetable and fruit crops our farmers produced each year. I worked for four years as a family and marriage counselor. Then I worked two years at my county office as the supervisor of the Child Abuse and Neglect Office. I worked 23 years for the State's contract office to recruit private agencies to provide social services to needy folks. Finally, I worked ten years in the Office of Refugee Services as a grant writer and supervisor.

Mike Luea with clients and staff, Ecuador

Mike Luea, Baptism Sponsor, Ecuador

Pat McDonnell '65

Pat McDonnell came to Notre Dame from Detroit. He played attack on the first Irish lacrosse team, recording 3 goals and 7 assists in his two-year career. Pat graduated in 1965 with a BA in Business. He was a Marine officer and spent a tour as a platoon leader in Vietnam. Discharged as a Captain in 1968 Pat had a long career in accounting and consulting. He is now retired.

Marine Captain Serves as Platoon Leader in Vietnam

In the fall of 1961, I was attending a small Catholic college that was basically a fifth year of high school. One weekend – I think it was the Syracuse game -- I visited a high school buddy at Notre Dame and concluded that I was wasting my time anywhere else.

I transferred, but found my sophomore year challenging, both academically and personally. I was lonely having lived off campus before rooming with a guy, who, along with his Zahm Hall buddies played endless games of bridge. Spring of 1963 found me bored and well on the way to becoming a dorm rat.

That all changed with the infamous note in the Huddle announcing the formation of a Lacrosse Team. No experience needed!! *Wow, that was for me!!* It was a life changing moment. That first spring was spent confronting the mysteries of passing, catching and fielding ground balls. Fortunately, we had a few prep school, Long Island and Baltimore guys as teachers. I was committed from day one.

The best part was "Boomer" Jack Tate -- my first mentor. Fair but demanding. *"Let's see who can take a hit!"* Notre Dame is among the major events of my life, and lacrosse was the highlight – and Boomer made it happen.

Our first games were in Colorado in spring, 1964. The sky was blue over CSU and the temperature was in the 60s. On game day, one of our new girlfriends looked out the west-facing glass wall of the Student Union and asked, *"What time is the game?"* When told, she said, *"You guys are screwed. See that?"* Dark clouds were clearing the mountains and we played that first game in a howling blizzard. We won and I got an assist. It was the first lacrosse game most of us had seen.

The next day found us again in 60-degree weather in Boulder. The CU guys were arrogant, sun tanned California skiers whose disdain was palpable. I was among those standing with Boomer when their captain approached and told him that the field had to be plowed and the tab was $700, which he offered to split. Boomer responded, *"Loser pays."* We killed them, which was fortunate, since we didn't have $700.

My career moment came quickly in our next game – Ohio Wesleyan – where I scored *The Goal* in an 8 to 1 loss. Fame is fleeting.

That was the highlight of my un-remarkable career, but I didn't care. I belonged and had adventures with great guys. When asked about arrival time for a Saturday game, our response was *Thursday!* Our strategy was mayhem. I still proudly sport a cauliflower ear and scarred knees and shins. Opponents learned to be wary of ground balls. It was fun!!

After reading Leon Uris' *Battle Cry* and seeing too many John Wayne war movies, I had concluded that the Marine Corps was my next challenge. I thrived. Amidst the yelling, stress and chaos of that first of two six-week sessions at Quantico in the summer of 1964, I quickly adapted to the pressure. The next summer was a repeat and I was commissioned in September 1965. After almost five semesters with Boomer, I was physically and mentally prepared for everything the Marine Corps threw at me including 1967, where I served as a platoon leader and company executive officer on the DMZ in Vietnam.

Those of us who graduated in the mid '60s were "fortunate" in immediately being confronted with Vietnam. It was unique compared to those who came a few years before and most since. Some take a lifetime to learn what we learned about leadership, responsibility and decision making in mere months. The Marine Corps was what I expected – challenge, responsibility, sense of accomplishment and occasional terror. I was mentored by experienced officers and sergeants who held us to high standards. We would rather have died than disappoint them or our young Marines.

Typical was the advice of a sergeant: *"Lieutenant, don't worry about winning their respect. We have trained that into them. All you need to worry about is losing it because if you do, you won't get it back."* Another suggestion became a valuable lesson in planning and decision making. *"If you can't eat it, drink it or shoot it, don't pack it because where you're going you won't need it."* Focus on the relevant. The result of practice and mentoring was confidence in thinking, acting and deciding, often under professional or time pressure.

I completed my Marine Corps tour in August 1968 as a Captain, obtained an MBA at Michigan, and married my precious wife of over 50 years whom I had met at Rehoboth Beach earlier that summer. The moral foundation of Notre Dame and the lessons of Boomer and the Marine Corps equipped me for my life's work as a CPA solving problems and leading clients, people, offices, regions and, finally, the audit practice at one of the large accounting firms. A generation of accountants was exposed to the lessons I had learned from those who supported and mentored me through those years.

I have been blessed with a wonderful wife, three sons and twelve grandkids -- most of whom play, will play or have played lacrosse better than I ever did.

All thanks to Boomer and my lacrosse teammates.

Go Irish!

Pat McDonnell at the DMZ April '67

Jack Pascal '65

New Yorker Jack "Jocko" Pascal played midfield on ND's first lacrosse team. He served with the Marines in Vietnam and followed with a career in finance, including stints in the Middle East

---

Marine Lieutenant Finds Pipe Tobacco in Vietnam

I grew up in Queens and went to Saint Francis Preparatory School in Brooklyn, NY. As the name says, it was preparing students to go a university. There seemed to be two career paths to follow: go to college or join the Marine Corps and return for a career as a New York policeman or fireman. In hindsight both paths seem to lead to Vietnam during that period. Much to my surprise my grades and SAT scores were good enough to be accepted to Notre Dame. For years after getting into ND I assumed they must have needed someone from New York to fill out a geographic quota. A few observations after a few days at Notre Dame: everyone I met was smart, or seemed smart, and had been captain of some team in high school, which leads me to the lacrosse team.

I had been a reasonably good runner in high school and decided I would try out for the track team at Notre Dame. I went over to the Field House and told a guy who looked like he was in charge that I wanted to try out for the team. He said, "Go over there and get some shorts and a tee shirt" and, I was on the team. Well, I liked running, but in my junior year I was saved by the now famous message posted in the Huddle announcing the formation of a Lacrosse Team. The thing that was most amazing about the first meeting was that it seemed that a 100 people showed up and the vast majority had never seen a game much less played in one. One of the things that I recall most about the early days was at one of the first practices at the football stadium Jack "Boomer" Tate lead us through 1,000 jumping jacks and then running the steps at the stadium. Even if we did not know that much about the game we were going to be in good shape. The thing I remember about "Boomer" was he always had a smile on his face, but it became a joyous smile when he flattened some attackman who was trying to score a goal, whether in a game or practice.

Our first game was against Colorado State University in 1964. We took a train to Colorado overnight and met the captain of CSU and a few of the other players when we arrived to get our rooms sorted out. To me, they all looked like graduate students that had been offensive linemen. Well, it began to snow at game time, and we won the first lacrosse game that was ever played by ND.

The second game was against Colorado University. We arrived in the evening and it snowed most of the night. There were some suggestions by CU of canceling the game because the field needed to be cleared off. No way was it being cancelled even if we had to shovel it ourselves. The cost was $600. They suggested we split the cost, but either Boomer or

Jim "Hollywood" Salscheider said, "loser pays". In no way could we cobble together $300 or $600 between us. Thank God we won. We were now 2-0 and thinking of greater glory in the Midwest. Amazingly we wound up with a winning record our first year.

Our style of play for 1964-65 was to create mayhem and aggressive play to offset our lack of ball handling skills especially in the midfield. The rules then allowed for a lot more body contact and it was not unusual to find an opponent left on the ground after taking a shot or fighting for a loose ball.

One of the most amazing things about the lacrosse team was that it was truly a brotherhood. No one complained about not starting. We were all there to help each other. I know my life was changed by going to Notre Dame, but the lacrosse team and Jack Tate's vision made it a truly special experience.

Vietnam and the Luck of the Irish

I was in Army ROTC, which seemed like a great idea. You didn't have to worry about getting a job after graduation and you got paid. I was commissioned as a 2nd Lieutenant and went off to Armor Officer training at Fort Knox. I was then stationed at Fort Carson in Colorado Springs. The Vietnam War was starting to ramp up and it seemed that the Army's plan was to give you a year in the United States and a year in Vietnam. Of course, the Marines, thinking themselves superior to Army, got to spend 18 months in Nam.

In January of 1967 I boarded a chartered United Airlines flight from San Francisco. I watched Beach Party Bingo staring

Annette Funicello on my way to Vietnam. And so, begins my "luck of the Irish and the absurdity of war" story. Suffering from jet lag and the heat of Vietnam I was sent over to the II FIELD FORCE headquarters for what appeared to be a job interview. A Lt. Colonel said he was short three lieutenants at a tank unit on Highway 1. I figured it was best not to ask why he needed three Lt's. He then asked me if I would like to go there. Since I knew lieutenants don't get choices, I figured this was some type of trick question. How should I answer it? In the most enthusiastic voice I could muster, I said, "Yes, sir I would love to be a tanker and run road convoys up and down Highway 1". He said that he had to check with the Colonel Doyle first. Colonel Doyle, while not a grad was a fan of ND football and wanted to know how the team was doing.

Noting that I had majored in economics, he said the captain running the PX at the II FIELD FORCE was a Civil Affairs officer and his sergeant had just shot himself in the shoulder. I thought, "Wow this is one crazy war!" So, with the blessing of Colonel Doyle, and the luck of the Irish, I was put in charge of the Post Exchange (PX) and became the equivalent of 1st Lt. Milo Minderbinder of Catch-22 fame. For those of you are not familiar with a PX, it has all the beer, booze, electronics, etc.

Here's a story of how absurd wars can be. One day a general stopped by the PX and asked if we had any Mixture 79 pipe tobacco and told us to call his aide if we found any. Well, my sergeant located some in Nha Trang, which was about 200 miles away. The aide told me to be out at the landing strip at 7:00 a.m. the next morning and sure enough an aircraft comes out of the sky and lands on a dirt airstrip. The pilot is out of central casting: helmet, scarf, big mustache and asks why we are going to Nha Trang, I said to pick up pipe tobacco for the general. He was not a happy camper!

In 1968 I got a job at an investment banking firm in New York City. I worked on Wall Street for 28 years, mostly in investment banking and fixed income sales in New York and Tokyo. In 1996 I tried retiring. That worked for a summer. Then I decided I need to go back to work. Someone told me I could be a consultant and advise emerging foreign governments on financial markets for organizations like US Agency for International Development, the Asian Development Bank and the United Nations. For fifteen years I spent a lot of time in the former Soviet Union and then in the Middle East. As I say to people, I have been to most of the "Stans" (Kazakhstan, Uzbekistan, Tajikistan, Afghanistan, etc.). In 2007, in an effort to stabilize Iraq, a military and civilian "surge" was started, and I became a Senior Economic Advisor to a Regional Reconstruction Team spending two-plus years in Northern Iraq advising the Kurdistan Regional Government and later consulting for the United Nations Development Program.

Currently I live in Washington, Connecticut. I have been married to my wife Casey since 1971. We have one son and twin daughters. No grandchildren yet, but one of the twins has one on the way. I guess it is my nature to need a bit of excitement, so I have been a volunteer EMT for the last 10 years with the Washington Ambulance Association.

I can honestly say that playing lacrosse at Notre Dame was one of the great experiences of my life. We all owe a great debt to Jack Tate for daring to think big and start a lacrosse team.

Jack (Jocko) Pascal

Jocko Pascal (r) in Vietnam

Jay Smith '65

Jay Smith came to Notre Dame in 1961 as a legacy, the son of football All-American and captain under Knute Rockne, Clipper Smith. One of a handful with prior lacrosse experience, he played on the first ND team on defense. Jay served in the US Army and had a long career in education including a role in the aftermath of the Sandy Hook School shootings.

First Team Defenseman Has Long Career in Education

My father was a Notre Dame grad as was my mother's brother, who died before I was born. An only child, I grew up with ND stories and listening to games on the radio with my father, who would get so anxious he would have to go outside for a long walk. I was under no family pressure to attend ND. But after I visited the campus, when the time came to decide, I felt I was joining a familiar extended family.

I played lacrosse in high school at Loomis in Windsor, Connecticut. Tom Moran, a year ahead of me, was a big star at our arch-rival in an adjacent town. One day in late '63, while crossing the Main Quad, I bumped into him. He told me ND was starting a lacrosse team. I thought he was putting me on! He swore it was true.

At the first jam-packed meeting [100+ guys] in Nieuwland Science Hall, Jack Tate, whom I didn't yet know, was holding forth with messianic zeal that ND **NEEDED LACROSSE.** Only a handful of us had ever played, but that was no impediment to his bold vision. By the end of the night most of us had bought into the dream. The rest is truly history!

Since I had "forgotten" to turn in my extensive high school lacrosse manual and playbook, we made copies for everyone and used it as our text. Now we at least had a common language and concepts. Jack got Engineering Dean Harry Saxe to be our faculty advisor so our club could be "legal." Jack talked The College Lacrosse Hall of Fame into sending us a Bacharach Rasin Coaching Aids Kit (helmets, gloves, balls, nets, and sticks, hand crafted on the Onondaga reservation in upstate NY). Engineering students built our first goals.

I played defense in our first season and was elected co-captain for the '65 season with Jim Salscheider. Early that summer I tore up a knee in ROTC Summer Camp at Ft. Riley, Kansas. In late August my orthopedist said I needed an operation which would cause me to miss the first semester of senior year. Moving rapidly to Stage 3 of the Kubler-Ross 5 Stages of Grief, BARGAINING, we struck a deal: If I gave up lacrosse and "took it easy" we'd see how things went… so Sal became the captain and I became the coach for the '64-'65 year.

The fall of '64 was most momentous because it was Ara's first official season. ND was #1 for most of the year. At halftime of the final game, ND led USC by a score of 17-0. Then the PAC 8 refs hosed us. Final score: USC 20-ND 17!

One winter day up in the old field house balcony, where I was rummaging in Nappy Napolitano's storage closets of varsity football hand-me-down uniforms that we could use for the '65 season, I came across a warm-up pullover whose gold collar and "Notre Dame" across the chest in Gothic lettering made it familiar. Ara wore that top! I didn't know anything about branding then, but I decided to wear one as a declaration that this new lacrosse club stemmed from a mighty athletic lineage.

For me, the '64-'65 year was a graduate course in Applied Leadership and the responsibility of the "Loneliness of Command." As a junior I enjoyed being a teammate on and off the field. As a senior, I felt the weight of making short-term decisions impacting a team of 50 guys. At times my decisions strained or tore personal friendships. The hardest decisions were to limit playing time or to bench guys who were hurt but wanted to gut it out.

After graduation, I requested and received a deferral from the Army that allowed me to go to graduate school at Brown and be their freshman lacrosse coach (9-1). My ND teammate Joe Cooke '65 was my assistant coach. Entering Active Duty in June '67, I attended Armor Officer Basic at Ft. Knox followed by Defense Information School in Indianapolis and back to Ft. Knox to the Armor Training Center.

With orders to Vietnam for March '68, I was home on Christmas leave when I had a serious auto accident. I spent the next 1 ½ years in and out of St. Albans Naval Hospital in Queens, NY getting a leg put back together. I was medically discharged in June '69, 14 days before I would have truly become Captain John Smith!

I had a gratifying 40+ year career as a high school teacher and administrator in CT and NY, including 26 years as a high school principal.

After retirement, I was asked to come back on a temporary basis. Fate brought me to Reed Intermediate School [850 students in Grades 5-6] in Newtown, CT. On December 14, 2012, twenty first graders and six staff members were murdered in Sandy Hook Elementary School. That day six of my students lost sisters and brothers. Fifteen of my staff had taught there.

From that morning's lockdown to the following June, my task was to hold my students, families and staff close. I needed to listen, help them feel safe, project hope, link them to resources, and help us recover enough to re-emerge as a functioning school. I'm proudest of arranging to have two therapy dog teams in our school during every hour of every school day for the next seven months.

Whatever I was able to do to help Reed School it was because at ND I began my lifelong internship in the Loneliness of Command.

While writing this reflection, I paused to spend a day watching the History Channel's ten- episode marathon documentary, "Band of Brothers." While I have scads of other

memories, there is no doubt that contributing to the birth of ND lacrosse with my Band of Brothers was the most important experience of my Notre Dame years. I look back with pride that what we started over fifty years ago has evolved through constant fidelity, attention, and care to become the distinguished national program it is today.

Jay Smith with his "Ara" Shirt

Jay Smith (2nd from right) Brown Freshman Coach '66

44

Bob Johnson '65

Bob Johnson came to Notre Dame from Mankato, Minnesota in 1961. He played defense on the first Notre Dame lacrosse team and served in the US Army in Vietnam following his 1965 graduation with a BA in Business. After his discharge and graduate school, Bob worked in Product Development for Schlitz Brewing and Hallmark Cards. He then moved on to head marketing for several consumer product companies in the automotive and paper industries. Since retiring in Louisiana, he has followed his passion for woodworking by introducing and selling a line of specialty kitchen tools called "Cookin Wood",

Lacrosse First Teamer Serves with Army in Vietnam

To tell this story properly we have to go back to the main hallway of Loyola High School in Mankato, Minnesota sometime during the Fall of 1960. I had just been ambushed by my College Advisor who asked if I intended to go to college and, if so, why hadn't I signed up to take the College Entrance Examinations. I promised to stop by her office later that day to do the paperwork and then headed back down the hallway. Coming at me was Jim Salscheider with that well known toothy grin on his face. He proudly announced he was applying to Marquette. Just a few weeks earlier Loyola had won our Conference Football Championship and both Jim and I had been named to the All-Conference team, second team All-State too. As I remember, I told Sal, "Like hell, we're going to Notre Dame...so forget Milwaukee!" I'm sure I was suffering from delusional thoughts about a "walk-on" by the two farm boys from Minnesota who would then lead the Irish to yet another National Title based on Jim's pass catching and my foot! It turned out I was correct, about getting in that is, but why both those farm boys were accepted for the 1961 freshman class always eluded Jim and me. Over the years, we laughed about the scene in a staff room when someone turned over the next two applications and said, "Salscheider and Johnson, looks good to us!" what could they possibly have been thinking? I still remember being greeted at the front door by my mom with a letter in her hand and a tear in her eye, "My boy is going to Notre Dame"!!! (I really miss her and now I've got a tear in my eye!) Anyway, Holy Crap…what to do? I don't know about you East Coasters but in Mankato, Minnesota in 1961 that was a monumental event for two guys from the same class going to ND! Our school traditionally had put more graduates in the military or in the work force than into college. Amazing, Amazing, Amazing!

Later on, I find I'm standing in slush up to my a** at the Circle in my Junior year on one of those depressing South Bend winter evenings hitching a ride back to my off-campus housing. For those who don't remember, or even know, the Administration believed strongly that students who suffered from academic "insufficiencies" would be better served living off campus in "approved" housing where they could study their way back into one of the resident halls…. makes perfect sense, right? Before freezing I caught a ride to the corner of Angela and Dixie Highway where I jumped out to finish the trip on foot.   I shared the "pull- down stairs" attic with Salscheider and Ed O'Gara.   We had all achieved our "insufficiencies" during freshman and sophomore years and had found our hovel during a summer trip to South Bend before the new school year. After studying somewhere on campus, I was pretty well drained of enthusiasm and was asking myself why the hell I had signed on to four years of this! After crawling up the steps, I was greeted by Sal who said, "Bobby Boobs, we're going to play lacrosse! Until the day he died Sal called me that and I had to hold the phone away from my ear because he always yelled it during our Sunday calls. At that point in my ND career there was little to look forward to beyond football. Between the combination of an all-male student body, 8000 of us and a lot fewer at St. Mary's, never ending cloudy skies, and only five weekends worth looking forward to, I was open to trying anything new. Jim said, "How could it be worse than what we've got? Ed was smiling in agreement, so it seemed right but that was before I met a guy named Tate!!

Sometime after that fateful night, Jim and Ed hauled me back to campus to a classroom in the Chemistry Building, where we joined a bunch of guys who were responding to the bulletins Jack had put up all over campus. In looking around the room I was surprised to see so many people who felt the need to improve their lives by playing an unknown contact sport with people they didn't know. The room was filled with names like McDonnell, Sheahan, Settani, Joseph, Sillari, Sauer, McGuire, Cooke. But those introductions were yet to come. That night, we were treated to a talk by Jack and a Dr. Saxe, (rhymes with Lax) who would be our first coach. They explained what lacrosse was, (we definitely needed that info!) and how much fun we were going to have playing for

ND. We would all be getting "sticks", made by Indians somewhere in Canada, priced at an amount I couldn't afford, and when we got them we'd suddenly be a real team! It was weeks before those "bent sticks" showed up so until then we were subjected to workouts which rivaled the worst I had ever known; I grew to hate the stadium steps! Of course, I had yet to enjoy the physical and mental torture awaiting me during Infantry OCS at Ft. Benning, but that was for later. Come to think of it I volunteered for lacrosse and for the military ...there REALLY might be something wrong with me!

After all that exercise and telling myself I'd eventually be able to scoop the ball instead of plowing up all the practice fields and then "cradle" it for more than 12 steps before losing it the season was on us. Now I'd be lying to say I was any good but the neat thing was I was "good enough" to make the travel squad. No fancy transportation here, we were on our own and that meant arriving jammed into some really suspect vehicles. The classiest way to show up was in an Austin Healy driven by Tom Moran or Rick Sheahan, and others but we all had to scramble for a seat in anything headed our way.

I won't recount my game memories because no one wants to read "recollections from the sidelines"! However, my first boss at Schlitz Brewing played against us at Michigan State and was there for the bench clearing brawl in Lansing. The important thing is that lacrosse made my last two years at ND bearable, even more than bearable. As I have grown from a boy into a man (no laughing please), I've come to cherish the friendships that have survived the decades. Even though time and geography have made regular contact among us impossible, when we do meet or talk it takes only minutes to reconnect and to fall into the comfort of being with real friends. Although we didn't know it at the time, we had become part of something special and would eventually become proud of our role as "First Teamers".

As to my "ND experience", I'd have to say it was a very difficult four years. I struggled academically for most of the time and always felt the social life could not have been worse. Lacrosse was the bright light and made the last two years worthwhile. My academics even improved when I was forced to balance my time, and it was a great lesson, something that came in handy in later life.

Graduation was June of 1965 and I had made plans to begin graduate school at the University of Arizona in Tucson, no more South Bend winters for me! I packed up my Nash Rambler in August and headed west from Minneapolis to begin a new chapter in my life. There were a lot of hours behind the wheel on that trip and I had all that time to consider what I was doing and ask if it was really what I wanted. By the time I got to Tucson I had made a difficult decision that Grad School wasn't going to happen and what I really needed to do was face the fact I had a responsibility to serve in the Military. Much to the disappointment of my family I turned the Nash around and returned to Minneapolis to volunteer for duty in the Army. I had been prepared by Tate and his "physical approach to life" so Basic and Advanced Infantry training was a breeze. It was at Infantry OCS Ft, Benning that I met a "Tate equivalent" named

Reinmiller who thought his role in life was to break Johnson into a bunch of pieces. I kept thinking if Tate couldn't break me, I ain't gonna give this guy the pleasure of seeing me fold. Thanks Boomer, you were a great help.

After graduation I was stationed at Ft. Benning in an Admin role. I knew I needed to join a majority of my OCS class in Vietnam so I volunteered for my tour and was able to pick my assignment to the 1st Cav Division. I joined the Cav in October of 1967 while it was headquartered at An Khe Central Highlands. In the following year I had a lifetime of adventures that I would ever have experienced "back in the world". It was a witch's brew of laughter, turning myself in as a "missing person" to our camp MP's along with my hard-partying best friend from OCS or stealing the CO's Jeep and flipping it late one night for example, and terror, not worth recapping here. I experienced all this with some of the finest men, some just boys, that I have ever known. Sometimes I felt like I was herding cats when it came to my enlisted guys but, like the First Teamers, we fashioned a strong operating group and took care of each other when that was needed. I'm blessed to have had both groups in my life.

Johnson's Home on the DMZ

NVA rocket hits gas tank next to Bob's bunker

Bob Johnson on RR in Sydney, Australia

Will McGuire '65

Will McGuire came to Notre Dame from Wellesley, MA in 1961. As a member of the first Irish lacrosse team, Will played midfield and totaled two goals and three assists during his two years. Will graduated in 1965 with a BA in Liberal Arts and in 1969 with an MBA. He served in the US Army in Vietnam.

Lacrosse First Teamer Serves with Army in Vietnam

In 1963, who would have guessed that Jack Tate's flyers announcing the formation of a lacrosse club would lead to lifelong relationships, fond memories and more than a few life lessons: that hard work, practice and teamwork can overcome inexperience and, in my case, limited athletic talent. I'll never forget that first meeting on a bitter cold night when he convinced us we could learn a sport from scratch. For the next few years, lacrosse was to become a major part of my life and my biggest joy at Notre Dame. I will be forever grateful to Jack. My fondest memory is of the two one goal victories over Dickenson and Kenyon in 1965. (What a time we had celebrating in Kenyon's old pool house.) The club will always be special because we did it! No one created it for us, no one financed it for us, no one scheduled it for us, no one fixed up our twisted ankles for us. (Mine is now fused forever!)

My other "club" at ND was Army ROTC. For some unknown reason I chose infantry as my branch when we graduated in 1965 (maybe after a night at the Linebacker). I reported to Infantry Officer Basic (IOBC) at Fort Benning in early September 1965. The first Cav Division had just left for Vietnam but most of the assignments were still in the US. None of us had an inkling of what was to come. After completing IOBC, I was assigned to Fort Ord (an infantry school for enlisted personnel near Monterey, California). I learned the value of procedures and regulations, played a few games with the Palo Alto Lacrosse club and helped my fiancé, Marianne, plan our wedding which was scheduled for May 1966.

Unfortunately, a few days before our wedding I was reassigned back to Fort Benning to the 3rd Battalion, 7th Infantry, 199th Infantry Brigade (3/7/199th) which was being organized for deployment to Vietnam. We went ahead with the wedding but the summer and early fall of 1966 were spent mostly apart due to the training schedules at Benning and Camp Shelby Mississippi. Camp Shelby was supposed to resemble the highlands of South Vietnam, a little ironic as once deployed we never left the delta, except to visit the Brigade base at Long Binh, and never operated on land higher than one or two feet above sea level. We deployed in late fall 1966. (Luckily, I had applied to various graduate schools before deploying and arranged to take the graduate records exam in Saigon in March. I left Marianne with the task of picking a school should I be accepted. She was also pregnant with our first child.)

On arriving in Vietnam, I was reassigned to E company, 3rd Battalion, 7th Infantry (E/3/7) as its executive officer. I was to remain in that position for the remainder of my time in Vietnam, except for a short stint as company commander when the then company commander was wounded. The Brigade headquarters were at Long Binh Post. However, we almost never saw that post as our area of operation was in the delta south of Saigon. We operated with a South Vietnam ranger company, and one of my jobs was coordinating with them. Most of the days and nights were spent in small unit patrols (platoon and squad). Unfortunately, the Viet Cong also operated in small patrols in the same area along with some nasty "booby traps". It was the guys in the squads that bore the bulk of the work and casualties. It was my job to ensure they had the support they needed and comfort when things went wrong. Unfortunately, things did go wrong at times but there were also times of accomplishment when we repaired buildings, evacuated suffering children and comforted the elderly.

Mostly I remember it as a slow slog through endless canals and muddy bogs with daily helicopter excursions. I was not wounded, just a bad case of fungus in embarrassing places and constant irritation to my "lacrosse" ankle. As someone wrote: it was a slow walk in a sad rain.

I learned that the Vietnamese were beautiful people. The rangers that we worked with tried their hardest and insured that we respected the civilians. The rangers became true partners and friends. In some cases, I was able to meet their families. Most did not care who was in political control and, like most of the US soldiers, just wanted the crazy war to end. Remember this was 1967, before the Tet offensive and the situation became far worse for the soldiers and marines from both countries and on both sides. We could leave, the Vietnamese could not and to this day I wonder what happened to those guys in the ranger group.

I returned to the US in early September 1967 to Marianne and our first son, who ironically would become a career marine and hear of his first child's birth while serving in Iraq. In less than a week after arriving home, I was sitting in a classroom as a member of Notre Dame's first MBA class. (Yep, Marianne chose ND over Harvard and a few others.)

Since graduation, we have lived in five states and four countries (US; UK; France; and Canada). We have been married for 54 years, raised four children and have eight grandchildren. Most of my career was spent in information systems: development, sales and implementation. We have lived in Virginia for the past 21 years and rekindled our fondness for lacrosse. We are avid followers of UVA; the University of Richmond; and, of course, Notre Dame.

Will with his Vietnamese Ranger Counterpart

56

Jim Salscheider '65

Editor's Note: This remembrance of Jim "Hollywood" Salscheider was written by his longtime friend Jack Pierce '70.

If you visit the U.S. Lacrosse Hall of Fame in Sparks, Maryland, you'll find his name inscribed on its walls as a 2000 Inductee into the Southern California Lacrosse Hall of Fame. Jim's selection, in the words of the Hall, was recognition that he was "a truly outstanding player who played a critical role in the promotion of lacrosse and had a major impact on the sport as a player in Southern California." He had the same impact on Notre Dame lacrosse.

Bob Johnson tells great stories about Jim. About to confirm his acceptance to Marquette, Jim was persuaded by Bob, his Mankato, Minnesota High School football teammate, to apply to Notre Dame. Once at ND both became disciples of ND Lacrosse guru and founder Jack Tate and the sport became addictive to both.

On January 4, 2020 Bob and I exchanged stories about our mutual friend as we sipped Jim's favorite tequila at his memorial service in Lake Havasu, Arizona. We both listened as a squad of U.S. Marines give Jim a 21-gun send-off and final salute.

You see, Jim was a U.S. Marine. He signed up to serve in the Corps shortly after his graduation. His military career lasted about 45 days until he was honorably discharged due to an undisclosed medical condition that the Marine doctors caught during a physical. Jim had responded to the call to arms. He just didn't get a chance to serve for very long.

I first met Jim Salscheider at the annual Alumni v. Varsity game at Notre Dame in the fall of 1968. You couldn't miss him. He entered the game wearing a standout red-white-and blue "Captain America" helmet. He was tanned, fit and had a great right hand shot. He face-dodged well and seemed to score at will no matter who was assigned to defend him. And when he scored, he'd flash his toothy grin to at all of us. Then he'd go back, face off and score again.

Many of us had never met him before that game. After the game a small group of us shared several beers with Jim and introduced ourselves. Jim was the ND Captain in 1965 and left ND after graduation to seek his fortune out West. He told us stories of playing lacrosse in Los Angeles and impressed us with his tales of perpetual sunshine, hot tubs and attractive women. We were envious.

It wasn't until the following year's alumni game that Jim and I struck up a friendship. One that has lasted a life-time. His play on the field that year was equally impressive. As we stood around the post-game keg he asked where I expected to be serving when I got my Navy commission. He told me that if I ever was stationed in the Los Angeles area, he'd like me to play for his Los Angeles Lacrosse Club. I told him it was highly unlikely, but if I did, I'd be honored to play with him.

I was expecting to get an East Coast assignment, but Uncle Sam had plans of his own. I was assigned to an amphibious assault ship on the West Coast and I played with Jim in Los Angeles for three years. Those years were memorable, both on and off the field.

Jim lived on the beach in Playa Del Ray with his large Black Lab, Pepper, who had lived with him at ND. We had lots of post-game celebrations at Jim's house. By this time, Pepper was getting old, but was still very friendly. When he wagged his tail, he would strike the wall so hard that it would bleed, leaving a two-foot high red lines on the interior walls of Jim's house. Jim also loved African tortoises. Big tortoises. They would dig tunnels under the patios of Jim's houses and disappear for days, until they got hungry for Jim's meals of fresh vegetables and would then surface for a feast.

Jim was also an excellent lacrosse recruiter. We had a talented team that enjoyed much success on the field. Our one potential weakness was at goalie. Jim urged me to recruit '71 N.D. Captain Jerry Kammer who eventually played with us after driving across the country from Baltimore. Jim lured Jerry to California with the promise of a job. He forgot to tell Jerry that his new job would be at "Olympus Burger" a 20-mile drive north from Long Beach where Jerry lived at my house.

Jim had a significant impact on my life. In 1975 I had applied to law schools on the East Coast where I expected to return. Jim asked me if I had considered applying to Hastings College of Law in San Francisco. I had not. He extolled the virtues of Hastings and casually mentioned that Marvin Anderson, the father of his business partner, was the Dean at Hastings. Besides, he said, as a California resident, my tuition would be $375 per semester. I found his arguments to be persuasive.

For a period of seven years, Jim and I were fierce competitors. His L.A. team would win the Southern California championship, and my San Francisco Lacrosse Club would win the Northern championship. We met most of those years the finals of Western State tournaments and in the state championship and we would bet a dinner on every one of those games. One of us never lost a bet.

As the years went on, our friendship grew stronger. He was the co-presenter, with my son Jordan, at my 2014 HOF Induction ceremony. He would visit me on his trips to the Bay Area. Each year, I would travel to Lake Havasu to celebrate his birthday.

His 76th birthday celebration was in April, 2019. Four members of the 1973 11-1 ND team joined us at Lake Havasu for the celebration. In his honor we all wore "Hollywood" Salscheider lacrosse shirts emblazoned with his number, 55, which were made for the occasion. Jim and his wife, Cindy took us "up river" for a tour of the river canyons on his pontoon boat. That weekend, at a dinner, he was made an Honorary Member of the 1973 team which boasted an ND record that neither of our teams had achieved. Jim was truly touched by the award.

Plans for his 77th birthday never came to fruition. After a series of strokes, he died suddenly on November 16, 2019.

Part of his ashes will be scattered at Notre Dame in the spring of 2022 at a date yet to be determined.

Jim Salscheider's enthusiasm for life and lacrosse had an impact on almost everyone who came into contact with him. And I was one of them.

Sal with Pepper

Jim with Jack Pierce

Tom Moran '65

Tom Moran came to ND from Weathersfield, CT in 1960. One of a handful of men with prior lacrosse experience, he scored the first goal in program history. He tallied 10 goals and 7 assists in that first season. Following graduation Tom served on destroyers in the South Pacific and Vietnam. He and Laura are retired and living in Connecticut.

The Story of the First Goal in ND Lacrosse History

My love affair with lacrosse started when I was 15. At the time, I was living in rural Connecticut and my aspirations in life were for a job at a gas station, a street rod, and a girlfriend. After I finished ninth grade, my parents wanted me to transfer to private day school for boys. Not what I had in mind, but in my household one normally did what dad and mom wanted. I remember looking out the window during the initial interview at the new school and seeing guys my age running around in the snow, beating on each other with what appeared to be big wooden sticks. I asked what they were doing, and the interviewer told me they were playing a game called lacrosse. I thought it looked like a fun thing to do and was immediately sold on the new school. I enrolled at the private school the following fall, joined the lacrosse team, and played until I graduated. During the offseason, I filled my free time with more genteel activities like football and wrestling.

I arrived at ND in the fall of 1960 and enrolled in the Civil Engineering program. To say the least, I was a challenged student. The low point of my ND experience came during sophomore year, when I flunked math. A high point came when I saw a notice in the Huddle posted by Jack "Boomer" Tate, announcing the formation of a club for the then obscure sport of lacrosse. From that first meeting, Boomer put together a club and program that seemed to have little chance of success but that managed to grow and thrive, due mostly due to his own force of will. As I recall, there were only four guys (Smith, Findley, Carson, and myself) who had ever played the sport. it was an opportunity to do something I knew I would actually be good at, to join a Brotherhood whose members would support each other, work toward a common goal, and have a lot of fun along the way.

I had accumulated groups of friends from dorm clusters, my major, and Navy ROTC. But the most fun and the best friends came from the lacrosse club. We have all heard many stories about the game experiences and road trips. They are all interesting, and some are even true.

The adventure really started in March 1964, when we took on Colorado State for our first game. I still remember early in the game making my final approach to the goal with my trusty old stick from high school, cradling the orange game ball. The stick did what it knew how to do and propelled the ball toward the net. I saw it fly past the goalie's ear and the net pop signaling a score. We had proven that it could be done! That was goal #1 in game #1. Notre Dame lacrosse was on the board and in the books. A new chapter of ND athletics had been opened. We had shaken down a little thunder from the sky on that mile high field. My tenure in the lacrosse program was limited to that two-game trip to Colorado and the following spring season at ND. I graduated in January 1965, after taking nine semesters to complete what most were able to do in eight.

Because I had been in the Navy ROTC program, I made an instantaneous post-graduation transition from student to sailor. I had wanted to stay on campus and play in the 1965 lacrosse season, but the Navy needed fresh meat for the war machine and I was shipped out to USS Morton (DD 948) in San Diego, CA. Over the next five years, I made three combat deployments to the Western Pacific on the USS Morton and USS Somers (DDG 34).

One of our primary missions was to act as a floating artillery platform, providing gunfire support to our Army and Marine Corps brothers down South (against armed bad guys), and logistic interruption bombardment operations up North (against well-armed bad guys). Our efforts were seldom appreciated by the opposition and we received a lot of return fire.

Feeling the concussion from the explosions and hearing the shrapnel rattle off the sides of our little Tin Can, as destroyers are appropriately known, was unnerving at best. A destroyer is essentially a 400-foot tube full of fuel tanks, ammunition magazines, high-pressure steam systems, and 240 souls all bundled in a 1/2-inch steel wrapper. A hit in any of those vulnerable areas could have been catastrophic. We had a lot of near misses but fortunately never a direct hit. I had become used to defensemen on the lacrosse field chasing me around and trying to hurt me with their big sticks, but I could never get comfortable with the North Vietnamese Army shooting at my ship with their big guns and trying to kill me.

Another mission was to provide search and rescue services to Navy aviators (think Pete Sillari, Ed O'Gara) who were not able to make it back to their aircraft carriers. A third mission was to act as a goalkeeper (think Bill Joseph) and intercept attacking ships or aircraft attempting to get to the carriers. None of this was what one would refer to as calming work and I was ready to go home when my time was done.

My participation in the war was essentially an arm's-length experience. I never saw, heard, smelled or touched any member of the opposition, unless I unknowingly sat next to one of them in a bar in Hong Kong, where both sides went for R&R. Nobody on my ships ever shed blood because of enemy fire, but we did lose two men overboard who were never recovered. My experience could have been very different had the person who gave me my assignment made a different pen stroke and sent me elsewhere. In the military you did what you were told, and I did the job I was given.

I realize that military service is not the right choice for everybody, but it was the choice I made and I have no regrets. The Navy was good to me and the experience led me to the perfect wife, a wonderful family, and a rewarding career. My wife is still perfect and we are looking forward to our 49th anniversary this summer. We have two wonderful daughters who are paired with equally wonderful sons-in-law, and four terrific grandchildren. Everybody is thriving. I still have that old stick and we sit by the fire together and think about the Glory Days with the Brotherhood. Every once in a while, I think I see the stick twitch. It must remember Game 1, Goal 1, just like I do.

Tom Moran (left) with actor Robert Stack, Tonkin Gulf

Tom Moran: We were in company with an aircraft carrier, and a USO group of two entertainers and their support staff was visiting the ships in the Tonkin Gulf. The aircraft carrier with a crew of 4-5,000 got Nancy Sinatra ("These Boots Are Made For Walking") and our destroyer with a crew of 340 got Robert Stack (Elliot Ness on TV's "The Untouchables"). Stack and I spent a lot of time together and struck up somewhat of a friendship. He invited me to visit him at his home in Hollywood when we got back. I did take him up on his invitation and enjoyed a delightful lunch with he and his wife at their home.

THOMAS
MORAN

USS Somers, Naval Gunfire Support off of DaNang showing spent gunpowder cans

USS Somers DDG 34

Dr. Carl Giombetti '65

Carl Giombetti came to ND in 1961 from Scarsdale, NY. He played midfield on the first lacrosse team, scoring three goals and five assists in his career. Carl received his medical degree from Philadelphia College of Osteopathic Medicine. He was drafted out of his pediatric residency and served two years in the Army treating military dependents as an Army Major. He continues to practice as a pediatrician.

Former Midfielder Cares for Military Dependents as Army Doc

Thank you for giving me the opportunity to share my thoughts about my ND Lax days. I was on the initial group of guys who responded to that infamous note on campus asking if anyone was interested in learning or signing up for a Lacrosse Club, meet at Nieuwland Science Hall Sunday around 2:00 pm.

A little background: I was in my brother-in-law's garage the previous summer and I saw this strange "thing" in the corner. I asked him, what is that? He was from Long Island and told me it was a lacrosse stick and that he had played in high school and at Rensselaer Polytechnic Institute (RPI) in Troy, NY. He was a very good attackman and briefly told me about the game. He still had cleat marks on his chest from when they played Syracuse, and Jim Brown just marched down the field, impossible to stop.

So when I saw the invite to learn about lacrosse at ND I thought I would check it out. I was not a big guy, and in high school I ran track, but loved all sports. Jack Tate's charisma and love for the game pulled me right in. Those two years were the most memorable times for me at ND. It helped me grow and mature physically (I hated running up and down the stadium steps, especially in the winter) and it gave me focus to pick my goal and stick with it. I was amazed they let me continue to participate for I had NO lacrosse skills but had fun trying to learn.

As we all remember the games were "interesting", but the road trips were memorable. Others have talked about the "snow game" with Colorado University and the loser would pay for clearing the field (I think it was around $700.00) and we won the game. We actually won the first two games in Colorado, so we were flying high as we returned to campus. I also remember how we were humbled when we played Denison and the papers had in bold print how they whipped the great Notre Dame.

There were a great bunch of guys on the team, some with lacrosse skills, but most of us were very green rookies throwing the ball in many directions. Early on, if we had three passes in a row some of us were ecstatic. It was when we went on an East Coast road trip and saw the Navy team scrimmage that I realized what good lacrosse was about. I could not believe how they passed the ball around in a circle, so fast and so accurate. I did play in games and even contributed with a few goals and assists. Those years helped in my maturation and eventually guided me to where I am now.

I became a Pediatrician and am still practicing outside of Philadelphia, PA. I spent two years (1971-1973) in the US Army at the Pediatric Clinic in Fort Campbell, KY. They needed Pediatricians to care for the dependents of the soldiers who were in Vietnam. It was a great learning experience for my trade, as we did all the Pediatric care and did not have the luxury of having residents and interns around - that was us. I made lifelong friends in the two years I was there.

A bittersweet day for me was when we had the ceremony for Jack Tate and his family at ND, when the tree was dedicated to him for the GREAT work he did for ND and for all of us to create the ND Lacrosse Club. It will always be in my mind and heart and I think of him often, especially when I am at a crossroad and it has helped me move forward... usually in the positive direction.

Go Irish and Go Lax.

Will McGuire (51),
Carl Giombetti (66), Ron Kirtley (23)

Pete Sillari '66

Pete "Mouse" Sillari came from Concord, New Hampshire to play attack on the first Irish lacrosse team. After setting a club assist record (22 in '66), he graduated with a BA in Liberal Arts and entered the Navy, serving in Vietnam as a F4 Back Seater with 200+ combat missions and 200+ carrier landings.

New Englander Sets Assist Record, Becomes F4 Back Seater

"Dakota two one four, Phantom, ball, 3.2".

We were three-quarters of a mile behind the USS CONSTELLATION (CVA-64) at about 400 feet, closing on the flight deck. Ron Stevens, my "stick", a pilot in Navy fighter squadron parlance, had made the call identifying us as an F4 Phantom with 3200 pounds of fuel. More importantly he was acknowledging that he saw the "meatball", a visual aid to assist pilots making their final descent to the flight deck.

I was in the back seat, a dutiful "scope", or RIO, the Radar Intercept Officer, very purposefully keeping my mouth shut and my thoughts to myself to allow Ron to concentrate on getting us back aboard safely. I could feel my adrenaline spiking as I looked down the left side of the cockpit to catch a quick glimpse of the ball for myself in anticipation of the coming jolt when we hit the flight deck.

Navy F4s have no flight controls in the back seat. The *only* control that allowed me any influence over my well-being was the ejection handle. So, when things got dicey my focus immediately narrowed to deciding whether to stay or eject. With no stick and throttle to command, I was literally out of control. These out-of-control decision points peppered each mission. It was the essence of my combat flying.

In quiet moments between the daily adrenaline hits, what the Stones referred to as "my fair share of abuse", I would find myself pondering a recurring question, "How the hell did I end up here? How did a guy from small town Concord, NH end up sitting off the coast of Vietnam at 30,000 feet with people attempting to shoot him down any time they got the chance, and carrier launches and landings that provided spiking adrenaline flows that had rewired my nervous system?"

As a kid growing up in Concord, NH I had always wanted to be a Naval Officer. Now bear in mind this notion started about the time I was 10 and by senior year at Notre Dame I was no closer to knowing or understanding what a Naval Officer was or did. Still, I wanted to be one.

This desire to become a Naval Officer led me to pursue an appointment to the Naval Academy which resulted in an alternate appointment. It was clear Annapolis would not be in my immediate future.

My B Plan was to earn a commission by being awarded an NROTC scholarship to attend one of the 52 schools that offered Navy ROTC. Plan B resulted in another near miss, but at least I had narrowed my focus to 52 schools, ND being one of them.

Finally, I struck gold with Plan C. Blue and Gold actually. I had applied to three schools and Notre Dame had been the only one to accept me. All I knew about Notre Dame at the time could be summed up as "Notre Dame Fighting Irish football".

Once at ND I found my dorm room, 133 Farley Hall, got my class schedule, a meal ticket, a locker at the Rock and I was on my way.

Playing intramural basketball at the Rock was fun but it wasn't playing for Notre Dame. So, when the notices were posted about a Lacrosse Club/Team forming my interest was piqued. I knew lacrosse was a North American game, a gift from the continent's indigenous tribes but that was about it. Hockey on grass about sums up my view at the time.

All I could see was an opportunity to play for Notre Dame, to wear Irish Blue & Gold. What was there to decide but where to find a stick, a ball, some help in learning the basics, and when the first practice was going to be held. That meeting changed everything for me.

The University provided classes resulting in a degree. But I got my education from lacrosse – on the field playing and off the field managing club business.

I learned hard work provided a path for improvement. Practices highlighted the value of perseverance. Teammates revealed the blessings of friendship, loyalty, and brotherhood. And road trips: well, road trips were their own kind of eye-opening education for a small town kid… to put it mildly.

But the biggest value or benefit to being on the team was just how much fun it was. Yes, it was hard work, and no, no one ever suggested that running the stadium steps was fun. Hanging with my teammates, scheming on how we were going to get everything done, and competing with each other at practice for bragging rights was as enjoyable as it was stimulating.

Playing lacrosse was just too much fun. There were very few days I didn't look forward to practice because we got to play lacrosse - two-on-two, three-on-three, man up drills, fast break drills, full scrimmages.

And then came game time. Nothing compared to the fun of game time.

I lived for that moment in a game when I made my move behind the goal, beat my defender and headed for the goal mouth knowing that "Stork", long and lanky Cliff Lennon, would be in the perfect spot out front in the open space left by his defender who had slid to pick me up. "The Stork" was always there. It was as though he was pulling the ball from my stick to his. He made it look so easy and so effortless.

To hit Cliff moving to an open slot where he would quick stick his shot into the net before the goalie could even twitch was more satisfying to me than scoring a goal. Explains why I had so few goals!

I'm grateful to the University for the degree I received, for the means to earn a commission and accomplish my goal of becoming a Naval Officer, for exposure to new worlds.

However, the lacrosse team *was* my Notre Dame experience.

My friends were teammates. My schedule had to allow for daily practice. I moved back on campus senior year to insure I was available for club business off the field. Summer nights at home, after work, were spent improving my stickwork with endless hours throwing the ball against the brick wall of a nearby school.

I learned that consistent work is required to make a club and a team viable and successful. There is a relationship between hard work and a desired result. Being loyal to your friends, your teammates and taking care of each other is of the highest importance. "What though the odds be great or small" is not just a line in a song but an attitude to adopt, a tradition to pull on when things get tough. And perseverance is a practical and useful quality to develop.

These are all lessons that I still find useful to this day.

Certainly these lessons proved useful the day the Skipper of my F4 training squadron wanted to pull my wings because I was constantly getting air sick. I convinced him he just couldn't do that. I had worked too hard, endured too much, been sick too many times to lose my wings. And if he examined my performance, there was no drop off.

What though the odds be great or small Skipper, don't worry about me.

Lt SQ Sillari on being told to man Alert 5

200 COMBAT MISSIONS

Left to Right: CDR GENE GARDNER, LT PETE SILLARI, LT MIKE MARNANE, LT JERRY BEAULIER, CDR SKIP FURLONG: (Foreground) LT BOB CLOYES, LT GARY GEIGEL, LT STEW SCHMITT, LT PETE KIRN

Dr. John Walker '67

Johnny "Dixie" Walker came to Notre Dame from Shreveport, LA in 1963. He was a midfielder on the lacrosse team, recording a goal and two assists in his career. He graduated from ND with a BS in preprofessional, earned his MD from LSU in 1970 and served in the US Public Health Service

Louisiana Native Gets MD and Serves at Wounded Knee

My Notre Dame story began in my parochial school 4th grade when I sent a postcard to ND, requesting information and expressing an interest in playing football, I guess at the suggestion of my Jesuit priest/football coach. ND responded with a form letter and the school catalog.

I really didn't give ND another thought until my senior year in public high school, when I was already signed up with LSU and had attended a number of animal house fraternity rush parties. The few public school Catholics in Shreveport attended Sunday school religion classes. Our teacher there was a local businessman and ND alum, who helped me come to the realization that ND would give me a better shot at a good education. Plus a friend and classmate was awarded an ND football scholarship, so I rushed in a late application. I loved everything about ND: the great teachers, freshman PE encouraging you to try everything, intramural games, the

Rock, the library and the grotto, plus the spectator sports and pageantry (the band).

After getting cut from baseball tryouts, I wandered over to the lacrosse practice fields with Hank Cluver, George Dunn, and Larry Duke, and I joined the team. I had never touched a lacrosse stick before. But with encouragement and good coaching from Jack Tate, Jay Smith, Cliff Lennon, Pete Sillari and others, I rose to the rank of third string midfield. The coaching process was: see one, do one, teach one. And that's how a bunch of us learned lacrosse. I quickly saw how we managed a club sport with no funds. On a road trip to Denison and Kenyon we had eight guys per auto and our mentors showed us how to get a room at a Ohio motel for two and sleep at least eight in the room by placing the mattresses on the floor...slipping in two at a time to avoid suspicion and slipping out before dawn and forgetting to pay. I kept glancing back for the local police, trying to decide what to tell my mom if I ended up in a jail far from ND. The best thing about lacrosse was the culture of hard-fought games followed by a good party with our opponents, especially if they were buying the beer.

The ND lacrosse highlight for me was the Colorado trip of 1966. Thinking back, whoever was in charge of the logistics for our team for that crazy busy week gets a five-star A+ rating. We traveled to Colorado, played four games in four different venues in one week, plus provided accommodations, food, etc. We slept on the gym floor at Colorado College, a dorm room at the U of Denver and in the plush Visiting Officers Quarters at the Air Force Academy. I scored my one and only goal in the Colorado College game and got a huge hematoma of the buttock in the U. Of C. game. John Brandau and I delayed our return to ND one day to go skiing at Arapaho Basin. I added another bruise to my butt on that ski excursion.

I am a Veteran of the US Public Health Service 1970-1973. USPHS responsibilities include providing health care to the Coast Guard, Merchant Marine and the Indian Health Service, among others. I interned in USPHS Hospital in San Francisco and then had the option of Mekong Delta with the Coast Guard or Indian Health Service. My wife Anita and I discussed our options and after a five minute discussion we were off to the Pine Ridge Oglala Sioux Reservation for two years. The IHS and Pine Ridge were a good fit for us, and I confirmed my plans to practice family medicine. Along with five other neophyte doctors, we ran a small hospital, a busy clinic and 24/7 Emergency Room, delivered babies, and ran rural clinics on the Reservation. We had a great time doing it. We learned a lot about our Native American population and their long list of health and social issues. For special emergencies we called in an air ambulance and accompanied our patients to Denver Fitzsimmons Army Hospital.

We were not immune to warfare in South Dakota. The American Indian Movement (AIM) captured the Wounded Knee Trading Post in the winter of '72 and held it for months, surrounded by Federal Marshals. We treated both sides in our ER.

I'm glad that I was able to serve our country in the USPHS. I honor all of my ND classmates and contemporaries who served in the armed forces. My childhood friend and neighbor was killed in Vietnam by a land mine, and I honor him. But I was not in favor of that war and peacefully demonstrated against it.

I've been practicing family medicine in Louisiana for 44 years. Anita and I just celebrated our 50th wedding anniversary via Zoom. We have three children and six grandkids age seven months to 10 years.

My partner and I began recruiting a young family physician as I was approaching 65. After Dr. Smith joined our practice, I used to ask him how things were going. His answer was always the same..." I'm living a dream".

Come to think of it, I have been living a dream too.

John Walker, Public Health Service

Dr. Hank Cluver '67

Hank Cluver came to ND from Broomall, PA in 1963. He played midfield and defense on the first ND lacrosse team. Hank graduated in 1967 and went to dental school at Penn. He then served in the Navy followed by a long career practicing dentistry.

Defenseman Spends Night in Maternity Ward

My Notre Dame story begins in New York City in 1928. My father had been working for three years post high school to save money for college when his best friend, Otto Struve, came home from Notre Dame on break. Otto had been recruited by Knute Rockne as a lineman and that year he convinced dad he should apply to Notre Dame. Dad who had never been outside of NYC lived his freshman year in what was then Bronson Hall, the third floor of the Administration Building. Dad graduated in 1933 with a degree in Electrical Engineering spending his senior year living in 402 Badin Hall, more on that later.

As a child my first words were mommy, daddy and Notre Dame, possibly not in that order. We never went to games but I was fully indoctrinated in ND lore. When I received my acceptance letter in December 1962 I already had the required ND clothing. A mail order from "Brother Bookstore" required 6-8 weeks for shipping!

Freshman year I lived in Stanford and played Interhall football. After the season I received an invitation in my mailbox to join the lacrosse team. Practice then was on the fields along Notre Dame Avenue, the present Hesburgh Center. My high school girlfriend, now wife, had played lacrosse and I could throw and catch a little but had to spend many hours with Jay Smith who taught me how to cradle while running.

That spring I played middie but when it came time for the first, and historic, west coast trip my parents refused to give me permission, saying I was only a freshman. I was fortunate to make all the remaining traveling games, our first against Ohio Wesleyan. Everyone has stories of those early road trips and the games were complete with cold temperatures, mud and snow. All were fantastic experiences with a great bunch of guys.

On our way to a game which I believe was at Kenyon our car caravan got lost somewhere in Ohio and we regrouped at a gas station around 10pm. Seeing several cars and a group of motley guys gathering a passerby called the police. Upon police arrival we explained we were the Notre Dame Lacrosse team and we were lost. It was too late for us to call or check in to our scheduled lodgings. The police officers generously took several guys home, and called friends and firefighters to house small groups of us for the night. Three of us went to the local Catholic hospital and I woke up looking at two nuns shocked to see me sleeping in the maternity ward!

What I remember about the upperclassman, who comprised most of the team, was that all were friendly and supportive of the freshman. It seemed really cool that I had friends who were juniors and seniors. In the spring of my junior year we traveled west again to play in Denver and at the Air Force Academy. We arrived at the Academy still in uniform from having played Colorado College and were housed in the BOQ. Seeing the cadets around us we were a little embarrassed by our appearance at arrival and we all quickly cleaned up for dinner looking more like respectable ND athletes. Ah, the memories: Selling football programs, spring practice under the stadium, running the stadium steps, all 60 of them, and practicing on snowy fields.

In my sophomore and junior years I played defense, never a starter but I always saw playing time. The starters, Ragusa, Hunderfund, and Dwyer were all better players and I was looking forward to senior year when I thought I had a chance to start. I was living in Badin, yes room 402, my father's old room. In the first week of school Johnny Walker who lived down the hall and I would go to practice together. After two weeks I realized that we had acquired two freshmen defensemen from Long Island who were experienced players and I would not be a starter. I felt I needed to make a decision, how would I spend my last year at Notre Dame?

I was anticipating being accepted into dental school and while I loved lacrosse and the other players it consumed most of my non-academic time. I made the difficult decision that I wanted to explore more of the college experience and I told Matt Dwyer I was leaving the team. That year I actually did things like attending plays, concerts, and Friday beers with Prof. Frank O'Malley; looking back it was the right decision, but a difficult one at the time.

Dental school at the University of Pennsylvania was a four-year blur. I do recall getting married after freshman year and having our first son during senior year. Dental school was going well and in my freshman year I applied and was accepted into the Navy's Dental Corps Early Commissioning Program. January 1968 I was commissioned as an Ensign. We had weekly meetings with other newly commissioned Dental Officers and two weeks of summer duty; mine was at the Philadelphia Navy Hospital. Since we were already commissioned officers there was no basic training but rather a month at Officer Indoctrination School (OIS) at Newport, RI.

Upon graduation I was assigned to the Dental Dispensary Portsmouth Naval Shipyard, New Hampshire. Due to turnover and my time in grade, I was now a full Lieutenant; I was promoted to be the dispensary's Executive Officer. I know my Penn training, along with my degree from Notre Dame was part of the Commanding Officer's (CO's) decision in my promotion. My experience was that being a ND grad was a big deal to the Navy.

When I arrived for Active Duty my first CO, who was on his "twilight tour" told me to consider my time here as a residency. He also said that he would do all he could to further my dental training. That type of statement to a junior officer was unheard of in the military. I certainly took advantage of the opportunity performing procedures that were often reserved for dentists with specialty training.

My second CO was also on his "twilight tour". As a plus he was the base social director and as a collateral duty I was assigned the base golf officer. Yes, that was seriously my title since the nearby Air Force base had its own 18-hole course. I am now a little embarrassed by this since my ND military classmates were receiving orders that put them in harm's way while I received my Temporary Active Duty orders to appear on or before 0800 at the Quonset Point Naval Base Golf Course for a tournament.

I am very proud to have served in the Navy during the Vietnam War, even while many civilians protested and did not highly regard the military. Portsmouth was an aging New England town with only two major employers: the Naval Shipyard and the Air Force SAC Command at Pease Air Force Base so military members were well accepted. My father, who was an Army Major in WWII, and my wife were immensely proud of my service.

I separated from active-duty June of 1973, and returned to my hometown of Broomall PA with my wife and son and started a dental practice that I would enjoy for the next 38 years. No one during the Vietnam years ever said "thank you for your service". It was not until years later that I could appreciate how meaningful it was to have worn our county's uniform.

I have lived a truly blessed life. And life got even better when my two older sons went to Notre Dame,'94, '96. My youngest son was not interested as he stated "Indiana is really flat", and he would go to college in Vermont. Interesting note, he is married to a Domer.

The 25th Lacrosse Reunion at ND was a highlight event. It was good to see everyone again, all still looking pretty good, and sharing stories and old memories. The Saturday morning "Old Timers" Game was interesting as it included many much younger alumni. I remember by the 4th quarter us 40+ year olds were not playing as the game went from "no contact" to let's call it "chippy". At one time I was on the field playing defense with Dwyer and Hungerford with Joseph in goal just like old times.

The 50th Reunion in 2014 was beyond expectations and a large number of the '64-'65 team members attended. Two events that were memorable for the ND lacrosse community were the Jack Tate tree planting near the Circle and Jim Salscheider's tribute to "Boomer" at the dinner. Both were a fitting way to conclude 50 years of Notre Dame Lacrosse history.

HENRY
CLUVER

Hank Cluver and Carol at Newport RI (OIS School), 1970

Matt Dwyer '67

Editor's Note: Matt Dwyer passed away in 2004 after a battle with cancer. The Dwyer Fund continues to honor Matt while providing support to the ND lacrosse program. This essay was written by Matt's wife Barbara Dwyer of Lake Placid, NY

Lacrosse Legacy Serves in Peace Corps and Army

When Matt Dwyer was a rising high school senior, his father became employed as a partner in the second largest law firm in Syracuse, New York. This allowed Matt to apply to schools outside of New York State and not just Cornell where his parents had met when Matt's dad was a law student and Matt's mom was a PhD faculty member in psychology. So, Matt applied to Cornell, Columbia, and Notre Dame. Columbia lost his application. Cornell and Notre Dame accepted him. He picked the college that was farthest from home.

Matt had played high school sports as an offensive lineman in football, a long distance runner in track and of course he played pickup basketball. Lacrosse was not offered in his private Catholic boys' high school, but it was followed avidly in his home. Matt's dad had grown up playing box lacrosse with the native Americans on the Onondaga Reservation just south of the Syracuse city line. Matt's Dad, M. Harold Dwyer, played lacrosse for Syracuse University from 1928 to 1932.

Matt was looking for a sport to play at Notre Dame. In the spring of 1964, Jack Tate announced the start of a Notre Dame Lacrosse Club and Matt signed up. He found his second group of Notre Dame friends there, second to his St. Ed Hall friends. Matt loved lacrosse. He turned down his junior year abroad in Innsbruck, Austria to stay on campus to be player-coach, a position he held for two years with the Notre Dame Lacrosse Club. He went to every lacrosse reunion he could attend. He loved when the HOUNDS started playing in Lake Placid. We hosted an annual party.

After graduation, Matt was one of five of his classmates who was headed to Sierra Leone, West Africa with the Peace Corps as an agricultural development agent. Let me be honest. Matt had no agriculture experience. He loved his Peace Corps experience isolated far north in the small mountains of Sierra Leone. He and three other PCVs built a poured concrete bridge which connected two villages year round, which had previously only had contact for two months out of the year. He also worked with a British agricultural agent to introduce a new strain of rice that was more productive. In early March 1969 he was asked to leave the Peace Corps early on the rumor that he had been smoking marijuana at a party. Matt and five others who had resigned in opposition to his removal left together traveling for 30 days on their way back to the United States, visiting the Canary Islands and parts of Europe.

Matt returned home to find his second acceptance to Cornell Law School and his draft notice. The supervisor at the Peace Corps had turned his name into the Syracuse draft board. Matt was sworn into the Army and went to Fort Dix, New Jersey for basic training. It was there he came down with malaria that he had been exposed to in Africa. Matt also went to advanced infantry training and earned his sharpshooters rating. At that point, two captains, one a graduate of Georgetown and one a graduate of Boston College, pulled Matt's file and sent him to Vietnamese Language Training School in El Paso, Texas for 36 weeks. Matt would talk about the lovely young Vietnamese women who were the instructors. He was in a class of 100 men. Most weekends, he drove up to Santa Fe or Ruidoso to ski. He loved New Mexico.

From El Paso, he was sent to Monterey, California for more language training before being shipped out to Vietnam. Because he had been in the Peace Corps, he could not be in military intelligence. That meant that he could not be a field interrogator, which had been the purpose of the language training. He was assigned to Long Binh as a personnel clerk, REMF (Rear Echelon Mother**er). In this capacity, he instructed his parents to send him the combat orders of any person in the parishes on the south side of Syracuse and he would change the orders taking these men out of combat and into administrative positions. He said he changed the orders for about 55 or 60 men. Given his Vietnamese language skills, he got quite involved in a Catholic parish in or near Saigon. He loved Vietnam. He called Saigon an Asian Paris. He loved the wide boulevards and the women's native outfits which he said were flattering to any figure. He came home with multiple pairs of men's silk pajama bottoms that he wore out while in law school.

His LSATs were old, so Cornell required he take them in Vietnam. He said they were given in a hot Quonset hut. He then got his third acceptance to law school. He returned stateside in March 1971, flying to Travis Air Force Base outside of San Francisco in uniform. Once off the plane, there was no transportation provided to get into San Francisco, so they had to hitchhike in small groups. Matt said it was a terrible experience getting from Travis to San Francisco.

Matt was not quite in the world that first year of law school when we first met. He wore his Army fatigues almost every day. By the second year of law school he was acclimating to being back in the US. He got involved with the veterans group on campus eventually becoming its President during his second year of law school. He wore his fatigues all through law school. He also got Cornell University to adopt a policy that they would not have more than 30 days between semesters so the veterans would not have an interruption of GI Bill benefits. He was proud of his representation of the veterans on campus.

We got married on April 6, 1975, a week after his six years from enlistment was up. He was so happy he could never be called up for reserves. He was fully discharged. A few weeks later Saigon fell. Matt was heartbroken because he wanted to go back there eventually and felt it would never be the same. Matt was a quiet veteran. As he aged, Veterans Day became more important and more private to him. He would participate at our public school and speak about having served but never discussed it with the kids. He wore his fatigue shirts at home and always kept his dress uniform in the closet.

Matt loved Notre Dame. Whenever we got within 50 miles of campus, he would light up with a huge smile and be filled with excitement to be there again. Notre Dame as a physical place centered and calmed him. When we left Iowa on the day Waco, Texas blew up with the cult and FBI raid, we stopped at Notre Dame walking campus with the kids for two hours and praying at the grotto. Our calm was restored.

Matt Dwyer (81) vs Chicago 1966

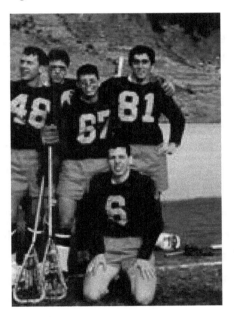

Matt Dwyer (81) with 1966 teammates

Marty Stoehr '68

Football hopeful Marty "Scarf" Stoehr came to Notre Dame in 1964 from Altoona, PA. He played midfield and faced off for the Irish lacrosse team and served as club president in 1968. Marty graduated with a BS in Aerospace Engineering and served in the Air Force for 20 years, retiring as a Lt. Colonel, and another 19 years as a DoD contractor supporting the Air Force.

Club President Has 39 Year Air Force Connection

The choice of college was easy for me: my dad dreamt of going to Notre Dame. He was the MVP of the Altoona Catholic High School football team in Pennsylvania where I grew up. But shortly after graduation, dad was drafted into the U.S. Army, captured after the Battle of the Bulge, married, fathered me, and never really had a chance to go to college. So, I became an extension of his dream.

Having started as both an offensive and defensive end in my senior year in high school, I considered trying to walk on to the football team. However, on one of my first days on campus I saw the layered muscles on the back of the neck of that huge man known as Alan Page and decided I needed to find another sport. When I learned that you could knock down opponents within 10 feet of a loose lacrosse ball and, in addition, would be armed with a hickory stick to check them, I found passion for a new sport. Like Len Niessen, the first lacrosse game I ever saw was one I was playing in at Michigan in spring of 1965.

After falling in love with Colorado during our team trip in '66 and being offered a National Science Foundation Fellowship by the University of Colorado, I went to Boulder to earn my MS degree. While there I played on the CU club team and was the high scorer with eight goals – needless to say with that as a stat we didn't win too many games.

Then it was on to the Air Force. During my first assignment, one of my tasks was to help convince a skeptical Pentagon of the military value of the GPS. I calculated potential savings by knowing precisely the location and velocity of the attacking aircraft as well as the target location, thus requiring fewer bombs and fewer aircraft sorties.

After that I served at the Denver ground station of the Defense Support Program which detects and warns of world-wide missile launches. I was part of a round-the-clock team of computer programmers that kept the IBM mainframes running at a time when it was rare to go 24 hours without multiple crashes leaving multiple blind periods during the Cold War. Assignments to the associated headquarters in Colorado Springs followed, including my lead of the justification of the launch of a new DSP satellite to replace a degraded one.

Next, I was second in command of a special AF detachment housed within NSA headquarters. One day during that time I ran into Bob "Rabbit" Noonan in the NSA cafeteria and we swapped tales (lies?) about our lacrosse days over lunch. A challenge during that assignment came on a courier mission to three sites in Europe that started on the day of Ronald Reagan's initial inauguration when the released Iranian Embassy hostages were flown into Germany. That altered our route and stranded us in northern Italy with huge boxes of "burn-before-reading" material with no local place to store them and no possibility of renting an Italian car big enough to get us anywhere – but we two Majors eventually got back on course and finished the deliveries.

Then, I joined a joint NRO-NSA center tasking satellites "of the highest national priority" – as my annual reviews said. (Even the letters NRO were highly classified then, but now they have an unclassified web site and I own a sweatshirt with National Reconnaissance Office spelled out.) One of the highlights of that time was weekly meetings of an Intelligence Community subcommittee that I attended and was always grateful for the up-front parking at Langley provided by my VIP passes.

My final assignment in the National Capital Region was as an AF liaison to a CIA group developing a new capability.

After that I returned to Colorado Springs and the newly formed Air Force Space Command as the senior officer within a vault of 20 people overseeing current and future AF special access programs. A personal thrill during that time was coaching our late son Brad on a high school lacrosse club consisting of four different schools with four leading scholar-athletes from other sports. In his senior year, Brad scored five goals as a middie in our semi-final state championship win, but sadly we lost the final. He went on to play for the CU lacrosse club and was their leading scorer with more than 20 goals his junior year – he was obviously a better shooter than his old man.

After 20 years in the Air Force, I retired for the first time and spent the rest of my career as an egg-sucking, snake-licking contractor for three different companies supporting the same programs I had been a part of during my service, but of course at a slightly higher rate of compensation.

Finally, in June of 2018, I "retired retired", as we ex-military folks like to say, from Booz Allen Hamilton, a consulting firm. That week was exactly 40 years since I had become an adult commissioned as a 2nd Lieutenant on Saturday, graduating from ND with a cum laude BS degree in Aero-Space Engineering on Sunday, and marrying Lucy, the Altoona Tomato, as dubbed by Matt Dwyer, the following Saturday.

Lucy, the Altoona Tomato and Marty

Tom Kingston '68

Tom "The Kingfish" Kingston came to Notre Dame from Staten Island. After playing defense for the Irish, Tom graduated with a degree in Liberal Arts. As an army infantry platoon leader in Vietnam he was twice wounded in action.

Army Platoon Leader Earns Two Purple Hearts

Growing up on Staten Island, NY and attending Catholic schools, my dream was to attend The University of Notre Dame. My parents and I drove to campus for an interview my senior year in high school, and we were immediately struck by the campus setting. I was accepted and my dream came true.

During my sophomore year I watched several lacrosse players crossing the quad carrying sticks. I asked Jim Caverly '68 about the game. I signed up and learned the "basics" at midfield as a sophomore, then switched to defense junior and senior years. Since I had a car, I was a driver for road trips in my old Buick, aka "the tavern on wheels," accompanied by Brian Kelleher '68 at shotgun and others depending on the roster. Hydration on the return trips was always a given. I enjoyed my lacrosse years and friends with whom I have reconnected with at class reunions and football games over the years.

After graduating in the summer of 1968 with a Bachelor of Arts, I received a letter to report to Fort Hamilton, Brooklyn for my draft physical. In January of 1969, prior to reporting to basic training, my wife Lana and I were married at Notre Dame.

I entered the Army in February 1969 and completed training assignments including Infantry Officers Candidate School at Fort Benning, Georgia. September 1970 found me in Vietnam assigned as 3rd platoon leader Bravo Company 2/1 Infantry, 196th Light Infantry Brigade. Our area of operations was a mountainous region southwest of Da Nang. The area was a notorious base camp location and infiltration route for North Vietnamese Army units moving into South Vietnam.

The winter monsoon season was in place, which meant a good day was when it did not rain, and a better day was when the sun was shining and we went without enemy contact. A typical operation began with a helicopter assault into a remote location to conduct a two-to-three-week operation searching for North Vietnamese Army units. While patrolling in the Heip Duc District in November 1970 I was wounded by shrapnel from a hand grenade. After ten days of recuperation, I returned to my unit. Heip Duc was the same area where Rocky Bleier '68 was wounded during the summer of 1969. Rocky and I shared memories during our 50th class reunion in 2018.

Late February of 1971, my battalion was repositioned to the DMZ. Our new home was the eastern most bases on the DMZ abutting the South China Sea. The tactics were different at the DMZ as the terrain was coastal plain with unlimited visibility during the day, giving the North Vietnamese accurate enhanced targeting capability for their rockets and mortars. Consequently, all combat patrols were conducted at night. A typical operation consisted of leaving the base in late afternoon, setting up a temporary location and moving into our final position under the cover of darkness. It was not as much fun as it sounds.

On March 22nd, 1971 as we were exiting our night position just south of the DMZ, we came under rocket and mortar attack. Unfortunately, the barrage was accurate, killing one and wounding three, including myself. I spent the next 21 days recuperating at the 95th Evacuation Hospital at Da Nang also known as China Beach.

I returned to Bravo Company and was assigned as the executive officer which is how I finished my tour before returning to the United States in September 1971. During my time with Bravo Company, we suffered an approximate 30 percent casualty rate (mostly wounded). I received two Purple Hearts. There were many sacrifices made in Vietnam, more than anyone knows, and we must never forget. I had the honor to serve alongside some real heroes and was proud to be there with them.

In 1986 the company began holding reunions every other year in Washington DC on Veterans' Day weekend. These events include our families and members of the families of those who were killed. The cornerstone event is a visit to the Vietnam Veterans Memorial, where we remember the soldiers from our Company who went to war and never returned.

After returning from Vietnam, I needed work. The banks were hiring ex-military officers. I worked for several large banks for over 30 years, including Chase Manhattan and Citicorp, managing global lines of business in international banking and global trade finance.

Lana and I have two children and two granddaughters, both of whom were baptized at the Log Chapel at Notre Dame. The family has attended many football games over the years, both home and away.

During one of our family visits nearly a decade ago, we had a wonderful encounter with Father Hesburgh at the Sunny Italy restaurant, where he and his brother were seated nearby. After he completed his meal, Father Ted graciously blessed my grandchildren. I thanked him for what he had done for Notre Dame and for our country.

I learned many things at Notre Dame while leading men in combat, most significantly to plan, listen, adjust based on the situation and always have a Plan B.

God, Country, Notre Dame

The Kingfish

DMZ, February '71

Hau Duc, Feb '71, Taking a Break on Patrol   Waiting for choppers to begin an op

Hawk Hill Dec '70. Grilling steaks and drinking beer!

Bob Noonan '68

Bob "Rabbit" Noonan came to ND from Wellesley Hills, MA. He played midfield for the Irish, scoring 3 goals and 2 assists in his career. Bob entered the Army following graduation, serving for 35 years and retiring as Lt. General. His awards and decorations include the Defense Superior Service Medal, Legion of Merit (3 Oak Leaf Clusters), Bronze Star, Defense Meritorious Service Medal (1 Oak Leaf Cluster), Meritorious Service Medal (3 Oak Leaf Clusters) and the Vietnamese Cross of Gallantry with Bronze Star for Valor. He is also authorized to wear the Army Staff Identification Badge, Air Assault and Parachutist Badges. He was the recipient of Notre Dame's 2018 Corby Award.

Midfielder Rises to Army Three Star General

The first time I ever saw the Notre Dame campus was in 1964, the day I arrived to begin my freshman year. Growing up as a Boston Irish Catholic, I always held ND in awe because of its tradition and its nickname, "The Fighting Irish". In high school I was involved in a lot of things and wanted to do the same in college. The summer after high school graduation I worked on Cape Cod with a guy who played college lacrosse. He wanted to play catch frequently and taught me the basics of throwing and catching. One day in The Huddle I saw an ad encouraging students to join the lacrosse team and so I did. Jay Smith was our coach and most of the team never played the game before they arrived in South Bend, but they all loved being part of something new and something that represented ND.

I vividly remember running underneath the stadium and up the steps above in February every year. Our strategy was to beat the opponent late in the game because we were in better shape. Most of the guys on the team played sports in high school so they bought into the culture of "what though the odds". Thank God that a few of them had played lacrosse. As a freshman, I was eager to be part of the team, even volunteering to play up top on the man-down defense. Here I found out that although a lacrosse ball is made of rubber, it really hurts when a shooter drives the ball into your chest. Over the course of four years, I enjoyed some great adventures, counted lots of guys as friends, represented our university, and even learned something about the game. It was also fun to be one of the guys with a barnyard moniker (Stork, Mouse, Camel, Rabbit, et al).

Highlights included crashing the Kenyon College English Department's Faculty swim after a game, a great Colorado trip in 1966 where we went undefeated, other spring trips in DC, VA, and NC; multiple car trips through Ohio on the weekends to play smaller schools, being elated in 1967 when we only lost to Ohio State's Varsity team by 2 or 3 goals (a sign that we could compete), fun games against the Chicago Lax Club, beating Georgetown and Holy Cross in a spring tournament, and many others. I will always appreciate our player-coaches who had the tough job of keeping us focused, arranging schedules, structuring practices, and so many other things. I don't miss getting drubbed by Denison every year we played them.

The day before graduation in 1968, I was commissioned a 2 LT in the Army, fully intending to wear the uniform for only the two years of my commitment. Things changed. A year later I was in combat in Vietnam as a member of a seven-man advisory team in the Mekong Delta. There, very young officers had to make some very hard decisions, often with no time to consult with their leaders. I learned that when stressed, people will fall back on how they've been trained, how they've been educated, and the values system that formed them.

Notre Dame taught me a lot, and to be truthful, most of it was not in the classroom. What I learned there were things that profoundly formed my life and career. I learned that we're expected to give back to society and our fellow man by being part of something bigger than yourself. Additionally, I learned that loyalty to your friends, institution, and others on your team provides an impetus to do well and to really care; you just don't want to let others down. Finally, I learned about resilience and much of that came from being on the lacrosse team. Often, we were the underdog, but we always fought hard, practiced hard, and maintained an optimism that allowed us to be competitive, at least physically.

After Vietnam, I decided to remain in the Army and over the course of a 35-year career, I leaned on these values in a variety of situations. Given a series of demanding jobs with ever-increasing responsibility, I had the opportunity to both command soldiers and to work in high level staff positions that demanded critical thinking and a lot of luck. Much of this consisted of building good teams that set very high goals and achieved them. Sound familiar?

I was in the intelligence business for most of my time, primarily at the operational level. After Vietnam, assignments included time in Infantry Divisions in Germany and Hawaii, two assignments at US Central Command, two tours at the Pentagon (one of those days was 9/11), and command of the Army's only operational Intelligence Command that provides worldwide support. I also had the privilege of meeting U.S. Presidents and senior congressional leaders, international leaders like King Hussein of Jordan, the President of Egypt, Kings and Sheiks throughout the Middle East, and other military leaders from around the world who gave me invaluable insight because I was forced to look at our country through a different lens. I've been to over 50 countries and as an ND Government and International Relations major, who could ask for more? In 2003, I retired as a Lieutenant General and the Army's Senior Intelligence Officer. Talk about luck of the Irish!

When I hung up my uniform about 18 years and 15+ pounds ago, I was privileged to join a great company, Booz Allen Hamilton. There I led a line of business that provided qualified people and innovative technology to military intelligence organizations across the Services, Combatant Commands, and within the Intelligence Community. I was also a senior advisor to the firm's Veterans Agenda, helping focus philanthropic efforts for wounded warriors and their families; a cause that will unfortunately not go away as these folks continue to deal with severe injuries. Many of our brothers and sisters will need help for a long time, a very small sacrifice that we should make for so many that gave so much. I'm now fully retired in Herndon, VA, but continue to do a few pro bono things to keep me busy.

I met my wife Diane in Germany where she was a Department of Defense school teacher for the children of Army soldiers stationed there. We've been married 48 years and she has enriched my life. We have two children and six grandchildren. Four of the grandkids played or are playing lacrosse. All of them are better than I ever was.

Go Irish

Lt General Bob "Rabbit" Noonan

Dick DiLorenzo '68

Dick DiLorenzo came to Notre Dame from Bishop Loughlin High School and Rosedale, Queens, New York in 1964. He played lacrosse as a sophomore but then focused on his engineering studies and ROTC. He served in the Air Force and DoD related fields following his discharge as a Captain.

Air Force ROTC Leads to Career in Defense Industry

Why did I choose Notre Dame? I was walking in the hallway, senior year of high school, and one of my classmates stopped me and said, "There's a scholarship you can apply for and I think you'd have a good chance of winning." It was the Notre Dame Club of New York. So, I applied to Notre Dame; and got an interview with the Club in Manhattan; and I was offered and accepted the scholarship. It was for $2,000 - four years of room, board and tuition cost $9,000 back then.

I made my best friends at ND through basketball - like Len Niessen, who was also a lacrosse player. During my second semester of sophomore year Len suggested I join lacrosse, so, I did. I never became really good at it but it got me into the best condition of my life - largely from running the stadium steps. But after about five weeks of lacrosse training - and some scrimmaging on an open field - I was doing poorly in my Science of Materials course, so I had to quit lacrosse. At

111

about the same time I applied for the two-year Air Force ROTC program and was accepted; my lacrosse conditioning helped me tremendously getting through the six-week AF summer camp in 1966. Wearing the uniform around campus junior and senior year gave me a renewed sense of pride, and I improved my grades big-time.

After receiving my BS in Mechanical Engineering and commissioning in 1968, the Air Force sent me to Wright-Patterson AFB, Dayton, Ohio, where I served as a technical intelligence officer until 1971. My job was to assure that relevant foreign technology/intelligence was provided to our cognizant R&D and acquisition personnel, particularly as it could help us in the war effort in South-East Asia. During this time, I also got an MBA from Ohio State.

I was then sent to Kelly AFB, San Antonio, as a mechanical engineer in 1971 with direction to assure that failure analysis of hydraulic hoses, fittings, and valves would lead to the upgrading of corresponding military specifications and standards.

At the four year point of active duty (September 1972), I opted out of the Air Force and used the G.I. Bill to "study" at a university in Aix-en-Provence, France for eight months before returning to the States.

In 1973 I was hired as a Defense Department civil servant back in Dayton and worked there until retiring in 2010. For the last twenty years of that stint, I was a professor at the Air Force Institute of Technology (AFIT) School of Systems and

Logistics. Besides teaching, this position enabled me to write technical papers for presentation in places like Beijing, Melbourne, Cannes, and Tel Aviv; and to meet world-class management and statistical quality gurus - most notably W. Edwards Deming. During this time I also got an MS in Aerospace Engineering from the University of Dayton.

In 2011 I was rehired by the DoD as a part-time professor to teach Design of Experiments, Reliability and Maintainability and other technical quality-related courses around the country. My official home office was Huntsville, AL - but I wasn't required to live in that vicinity. My wife Sharon and I bought a winter home in Naples, Florida that year. In 2017 I became "retired retired".

Incidentally, that high school classmate who suggested I try for that scholarship was Jim Hutchinson, who also attended ND and graduated the same year as I did. It was one of the most selfless things anyone ever did for me.

I met Sharon Wagner while I was a lieutenant in Dayton in 1969. We dated a few times before I was transferred to San Antonio. We got back together when I was back in Dayton; we married in 1975. She's provided me the best years of my life - and three fantastic children - and now six grandchildren.

Incidentally, Len Niessen and his wife Pat have a winter home just minutes from us in Naples. Sharon and I enjoy their company immensely. On Christmas 2020 I returned something to Len and Pat - the garter I caught at their 1969 wedding in Chicago!

Dick DiLorenzo (left rear) at 2018 ND Reunion

Chapter 2

The Hybrid Era '69-'74

As the decade ended and the new one began, things began to change both nationally and on the Notre Dame campus. The new President, Richard Nixon, inaugurated in January 1969, was still dealing with Vietnam. But the nation soon had other problems... the trial of the Chicago Seven in September of 1969 which had followed the trial of the Catonsville Nine, the latter of particular interest to Catholics. There were the May 1970 killings at Kent State. The Watergate break-in in May of 1972 and subsequent hearings dominated the news and led to Nixon's resignation on August 9, 1974.

The Draft Lottery was held on December 1, 1969 and it drastically changed things for young men becoming draft eligible in 1970 and later. Those who were lucky enough to get high numbers could go on with their lives without worrying about getting drafted. But even those with low numbers were looking at a winding down of the War. In January 1973, the Paris Peace Accords signaled the withdrawal of US troops from Vietnam within sixty days. When the last military unit left in March, over 58,000 US troops and 200,000 South Vietnamese troops had been killed in the decade long conflict.

On the lacrosse front, the STX company developed the first plastic head in August of 1970. Though it would take some time for these new hybrids – plastic heads with wooden shafts – to completely replace their wooden predecessors, a new era had begun. Photos from the Notre Dame Lacrosse archives first show a hybrid stick in the hands of Gary Riopko in 1972 while his co-captain Ed Hoban has the old wooden version.

But the biggest change for ND lacrosse came with the 1971 hiring of Coach Rich O'Leary, an outstanding lacrosse player at Cortland State in New York. This ended the era of on-field "coaches" and raised the level of the Irish program immediately. The following year, in 1972 the Club shared the M.C.L.A. Championship with a final record of 8 - 3 and finished the 1973 campaign with an unparalleled season record of 10 - 1. As Rich O'Leary noted in his report to Moose Krause at the completion of the 1972 season..."There were many players deserving recognition. Five players were selected to represent the M.C.L.A. in a game against Mt. Washington Lacrosse Club from Baltimore, Maryland. Seven players were also selected to play in the Annual M.C.L.A. North-South Game in Columbus, Ohio".

Co-captains Gary Riopko (Hybrid Stick) Ed Hoban (Wooden Stick)

Mike Satarino '69

Mike Satarino from Dallas, Texas, came to Notre Dame in 1965. He played defense for the Irish and was elected lacrosse club president as a senior. Mike graduated in 1969 with a degree in Management. He served in the US Army after getting his master's degree. After teaching business law and math at the high school level, Mike moved into administration and finished his career as principal of the Talented and Gifted (TAG) School in Dallas. In 2006 and 2007, Newsweek magazine named his school, TAG Magnet, as the nation's Number 1 public high school. When Mike received Notre Dame's Outstanding Educator Award in 2010, he explained his success with characteristic modesty: "I hire well."

Defenseman and Club President Wins Outstanding Educator

When our family moved to the house where I was raised, the first thing my father hung on the wall in my room was a Notre Dame pennant. I guess I just always wanted to go there. My dream was to play football for ND and to end up as the head coach of the University.

I was a member of the first graduating class from a new Catholic high school and I applied. I could not believe it when I was accepted. I had never been away from Texas except for one family vacation to New Mexico. I had never experienced snow. Thus began four years of new experiences.

I tried out for the freshman football team with six other freshmen and Rob Trost was one of them. I made the roster but Rob talked me into going and trying lacrosse. I did not know lacrosse and had never seen it played. We ended up on the field behind Stepan Center. I watched as they scrimmaged and then someone walked up and handed me a stick. I enjoyed the physical contact of the game but I did not enjoy getting in shape. I weighed 250 lbs. when I tried to compete for football and by Christmas break I weighed 185 lbs. My father died unexpectedly in May and had to miss a week during the season. However, the team voted to let me receive a letter award - something that I will never forget and for which I will always be grateful. In my senior year the team elected Rob Trost as its captain and me as its president. For four years I was privileged to watch the best defensive man I ever saw in Rob Trost and the greatest athlete I ever saw in Bob Morin. I scored one goal in my last game as a senior. I thought that was the nicest way to cap off my career.

I received a scholarship to pursue my master's degree at SMU. As soon as I received my M.Ed. I was drafted into the US Army and stationed at Ft. Ord, California. Playing a sport I knew nothing about prepared me for two things in my Army career:

First, at the end of my first summer in the Army, I was approached by a US Navy captain and asked if I had played lacrosse in college. When I said yes he said the Naval post graduate school in Monterrey was putting together a lacrosse team and wondered if I would be interested in playing. When I showed up for our first scrimmage, I was provided with a set of equipment. When I walked out on the field I was in the Army, playing for the Navy, and wearing a Marine jersey.

Later, the 6th Army tryouts for the Munich Olympics in 1972 were held at Ft. Ord. It was announced that the 6th Army wanted to field a European Handball team. As with lacrosse, I had no knowledge of this game or how it was played, so I volunteered. I made the team and played in two matches. We were eliminated, but, as with lacrosse, I scored one goal in my last match.

I reached the rank of Specialist 4th Class as a Physical Activities Specialist. The Vietnam War was drawing to a close and I was granted an early release because I wanted to teach.

My Notre Dame experience was exceptional. I met a group of guys and we became close friends. We still meet every summer for a mini-reunion. I am blessed that the only close friend I have lost is Rob Trost to cancer - I miss him every day.

Thank you for letting me write this. Besides being married for 48 years to a saint, having four children and five grandchildren, my Notre Dame experience was the greatest experience in my life.

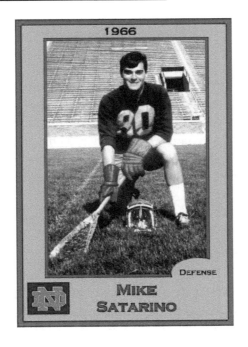

1966

DEFENSE

MIKE SATARINO

MIKE SATARINO

Ford Cole '69

Ford Cole came to Notre Dame from Long Island in 1965 and played midfield on the lacrosse team. He served in the Navy in Vietnam, then returned to ND as an ROTC instructor and earned his JD in Law. He had a long career in the FBI

Navy and Vietnam Vet Becomes FBI Agent

I was born and raised on Long Island attending public schools although I was raised as a Catholic. Babylon High School was relatively small and it did not have a lacrosse team although lacrosse was a burgeoning high school sport on Long Island in the early 1960s.

My father tragically died when I was seven; my mother was a schoolteacher at a nearby high school. In high school I was on the cross country and wrestling teams but my accomplishments were modest. I was only about 130 pounds in high school so football was not a natural choice for me. Both sports, however, kept in me in excellent physical condition and inculcated valuable lessons about tenacity and determination.

My senior year I applied to four colleges: Notre Dame, Rensselaer Polytechnic Institute (RPI), Alfred University and the State University of New York at Buffalo. My mother was lobbying for a Catholic college since I had not attended a

Catholic high school and the son of a family friend had gone to ND. ND was the only school I applied to outside of New York and since I had received a New York State Regents Scholarship going out of state meant I was passing up some financial aid. When I expressed interest in Notre Dame to my high school guidance counsellor, he asked me several questions about whether I was a practicing Catholic which, in later years, I found quite amusing since he was working in a public high school.

I was admitted to all four schools. I got a letter from the wrestling coach at RPI assuring me I would have opportunities to wrestle if went to RPI. While I was initially flattered by his letter, I quickly surmised that RPI, an engineering school, placed a low emphasis on athletics and that the wrestling team was all walk on athletes. At that time the RPI football team had a 30 or 40-game losing streak which the school representative joked about at a meet and greet. None of the other three schools sent me any communications about athletic opportunities.

In the spring of 1965 my mother and I drove out to Indiana to visit my uncle and cousins and then to ND for a campus visit. After my mother again expressed her Catholic school preference, she wrote a deposit check and we headed home. I was on the path to becoming a Domer.

When I arrived at ND, I signed up for Navy ROTC as a non-scholarship participant in the hopes of earning a scholarship through competition. I had competed for a Navy ROTC scholarship in high school but had been eliminated because I supposedly had albumin in my urine.

I am not sure how I learned about the lacrosse team. There were several Navy ROTC guys playing lacrosse: Peter Sillari (a senior), Drew Daly (a junior) and Chuck Metzger (a fellow freshman). Also, I knew Bob Noonan from Farley Hall. I recall Bill Joseph giving a talk to incoming freshman about how the team was a club sport that had to raise its own funds and that walk on students were welcome. I got my mother to shell out for cleats, a lacrosse stick and gloves. I was on my way.

As a walk-on player I was learning a sport I had never played, but the juniors and seniors made me feel at home. There were no fraternities at ND, but being on the lacrosse team made me feel like I was in one.

I was not on the traveling squad in the fall of 1965 but I enjoyed the opportunity to be part of a team sport. In the spring of 1966 a bunch of us B-team players got a chance to go on a road trip to Denison and Oberlin and play against their freshman teams.

Two experiences from my lacrosse experience stand out. In the winter we practiced at the stadium, running laps around the inside loop. While waiting for the practice to start one day, a bunch of us were sitting on the field level bleachers when around the corner wandered Ara. He chatted with us and asked about the team. It was sort of like the Pope walking in on a group of seminarians.

Second, I have a vivid memory of the spring road trip. In the highest traditions of club sport athletics, the bus broke down and we hitchhiked to Denison. After the game I saw two things I had not seen at ND: an open keg of beer on campus and coeds.

At the end of second semester of my freshman year I received a Navy ROTC Regular Scholarship which lifted a major financial burden off of my mother. However, it also required that I take a 20-credit hour load as a sophomore. After seeing a number of my freshman friends struggle academically, I made a sophomore-year decision to end my lacrosse participation as a sophomore. My one year with the team was memorable, however, and a picture of the '65-'66 lacrosse team sits in my home office.

My lacrosse experience unexpectedly came up again in 1976 when I was a third-year law student interviewing for jobs. I went up to Dearborn, Michigan to interview with Ford Motor Credit for a job. One of the interviewing attorneys had played college lacrosse and noticed my one year with the ND lacrosse club on my resume. Nearly all of the interview was devoted to talking about lacrosse.

I was commissioned an Ensign the day before graduation and went on active duty in the Navy. My first assignment was an aircraft carrier, the USS Ticonderoga (CVS-14), which was on the west coast in Long Beach, California and then in San Diego. I was a division officer, a CIC Watch Officer, and an air controller. In the summer of 1971 I received orders to go to Vietnam as an advisor to the Vietnamese Navy. After undergoing training in Vallejo, California I reported in late

1971. While undergoing Survival Evasion Resistance and Escape training I was "water boarded" which gave me a perspective on the technique when the government officially adopted it in the early 2000s.

Shortly after I arrived in Vietnam the DOD began reducing the active-duty force footprint there. In February of 1972 my position was eliminated and the CNO, Admiral Elmo Zumwalt, directed Navy officer detailers to try to give officers coming out of Vietnam their wishes. I was granted my wish to go back to Notre Dame as an NROTC Instructor. Thus, I was back on campus the final three years of the era of Ara. While at the ROTC Unit I struck up a friendship with Sandy Cochran, an Army ROTC instructor who was an assistant coach with the ND lacrosse team. At the end of my tour I attended ND Law School, graduating in 1976.

Those were some heady days for ND athletics. In 1974 Ara defeated Alabama for the National Championship. Not long after that, Digger Phelps ended the UCLA winning streak in basketball.

My first job out of law school was as a law clerk with a local Federal judge in South Bend, Judge Robert Grant, a double Domer. The clerkship led to another job with a Domer, Richard J. O'Melia, the Vice-Chairman of the then Civil Aeronautics Board (CAB) in Washington, D.C. Dick was a great guy, a former WWII Marine pilot and the President of the Class of 1939 at ND. He encouraged me to stay in the Navy Reserves. The job at the CAB was fun. But legislation had been enacted phasing out the duties of the CAB, and it was clear that everybody at the CAB was going to have to find a new home.

I had applied to the FBI while in law school and reactivated my application. I was selected and entered the FBI as an Agent in May 1978. I stayed for 23 ½ years with the FBI, almost entirely in the D.C. area. One of the perquisites of being an FBI Agent was being to able work out several times a week while on duty since we had to take an annual PT test. I used to jog across the 14th street bridge, cut across in front of the Pentagon and then return to D.C. via the Memorial Bridge. While jogging one day I bumped into Sandy Cochran and we caught up. On another day I saw Bob Noonan heading towards the Pentagon. I stayed in the Navy Reserves and retired as a Commander in 1995.

While in the FBI I participated in the expulsion of the Iranian diplomats in 1980, was involved in the Robert Hanssen investigation, interviewed several Supreme Court Justices and worked on undercover investigations.

I retired from the Government in 2001 and have been doing consulting jobs ever since. The cleats, the gloves, and the stick are still in the garage to remind of the lax days. And the team picture from '65-'66 is still hanging in my office.

Going to ND turned out to be one of the best decisions I made. Of the schools I applied to, it was certainly the most prestigious and its stature only grew after graduation. Because of my experiences with the law school, and my ROTC tour I was fortunate to see the university from a variety of perspectives. I got to know a number of professors and was fortunate to be there when a lot of change was occurring.

Notre Dame and its alumni connections certainly helped my career greatly. I will always be appreciative to those who helped me along the way. ROTC and lacrosse brought me into fellowship with truly great people. I certainly hope these traditions and values will endure after we are all gone.

Ford Cole (front, right) summer cruise '66

Chuck Metzger '69

Long Islander Chuck Metzger came to ND with experience as a high school defenseman. Following graduation, he served in the Navy in Vietnam and later became a civilian contract specialist for the Navy.

D-man Is Naval Communications Advisor To Vietnamese Navy

On arrival on campus in September '65, I was a wide-eyed 18-year-old facing a few immediate startup issues. One was momentous and relates to the then looming Vietnam 'situation' and what that might mean upon graduation. I quickly decided to join NROTC – that is, to play my luck and aim to go to sea in Navy khakis in lieu of being drafted into the Army and sent to Vietnam.   Also, on learning there was a lacrosse club, I signed up.   I had played lacrosse as a defenseman for Cold Spring Harbor High School on Long Island. My public high school was small and new (then) – only 93 in my class. If you wanted to play, you did. Lacrosse was a great decision on my part.   But, sad to report, I left Notre Dame lacrosse after my first year.

I really liked the low-key club lacrosse atmosphere, leadership by player-coach and upperclassmen, and the adventure involved, contrasting as it did with the strains and struggles of academic classwork and relative social isolation on the all-male ND campus.   One of the highlights was a fall scrimmage at Ann Arbor, U of M. How did I get there?   With no team-affiliated car available, I hitch hiked. We took bus trip to Chicago, Evanston, to play the post-college age members of Chicago Lacrosse Club (with free beer afterwards). We had a fine spring trip to Colorado, playing U of Denver, Air Force, Colorado College, and U of Colorado Boulder. There was a road trip to Kenyon College in Ohio. We had a plain vanilla practice/home field next to the then new Stepan Center; nearby were the Rugby guys. Not very many fans, no groupies. It was "just us".

During freshman year I applied for and received an available NROTC scholarship (tuition, books, $50 monthly stipend). This meant a regular Navy commission as opposed to reserve commission and an added year of service obligation (four versus three). Upon graduation and commissioning in 1969, I got my first choice posting to a destroyer, USS Warrington (DD-843), homeported in Newport RI. I was the gunnery officer on that ship. We returned from a six-month Mediterranean deployment in the first days of May 1970, about one day after Kent State. That was a shock. Not so many months later, in the late fall, I got orders to Vietnam essentially as a forward observer and naval gunfire liaison with the 3rd Marine Division in "I" Corps. (Oh blank, I had not volunteered!). That did not pan out exactly.

I wound up in a much different (and safer) assignment, green suited, as a naval communications advisor to the Vietnamese Navy in the extreme south of the country, arriving March 1971. This was after brief language training. I served at Intermediate Support Base Nam Can, aka "Solid Anchor". In February 1972 I rotated home (one month early), this time to a new construction ammunition ship, USS Mount Baker (AE-34), homeported in Charleston SC. I was appointed Navigator. After training up the crew at Guantanamo Bay, Mount Baker got sudden orders in December 1972 to transit the Panama Canal and relieve overaged, overworked ammunition ships STILL operating off Vietnam. This was in conjunction with the renewed bombing of that period (Christmas bombing). Fatefully, the emergency deployment orders were rescinded within a month. Effective July '73, I resigned my commission and left the Navy. A year later I went to work for the Navy as a civilian contract specialist in DC and retired in 2007.

I much enjoyed my return to campus for my 50th year class reunion and especially the opportunity to participate in the mini-lacrosse reunion. That was wonderful. Fellow defense player Mike Satarino was there. It was so great to see the guys. Sadly, Rob Trost, an absolute stalwart on defense, did not make it, having passed away a year or so earlier.

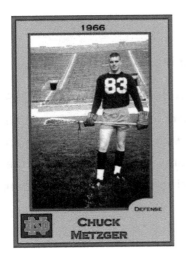

Mike Cerre '69

Mike Cerre came from Grosse Point, Michigan to Notre Dame in 1965. He played attack on the lacrosse team and graduated with a BA in Communication Arts in 1969. Mike served in the Marines in Vietnam. Starting as a sports reporter and news anchor for the NBC station in San Francisco and a contributing correspondent for NBC TODAY, he went on to produce and report his cross-country Working Journal series for ABC-Good Morning America and co-hosted PM Magazine in New York, along with documentaries for HBO and Showtime. He was a foreign correspondent for ABC News Nightline, where he earned an Emmy Award for his embedded reporting in Iraq, and currently is a Special Correspondent for the PBS NewsHour. Mike has been Documentary writer/producer for programs & series on HBO, CNN, CNBC, MSNBC, A&E, Discovery, National Geographic and Disney Channel as well as Strategic communications consultant for Fortune 500 companies, government agencies and non-profits on how great storytelling can generate great earned media.

Marine Vet Becomes Emmy Winning Journalist

I dodged the draft after my Notre Dame graduation in 1969 by joining the Marines. I was commissioned at a small ceremony in the Athletic Center with a dozen classmates an hour after my graduation ceremony. Who says Notre Dame lacrosse attackmen aren't opportunistic when they see an opening?

Guess I was a glutton for punishment. After the winter training sessions, running endlessly beneath the freezing stadium and up and down the stadium steps with the other spring sport club teams, I spent my sophomore and junior year summers in the sweltering, humid heat of Virginia training to become a Marine officer, along with fellow lacrosse teammate Bob Trost. (I believe he was eventually medically discharged.) I probably should have been as well due to chronic ankle tendon tears playing lacrosse and from a skiing injury in Colorado which was all my teammate Bob "Slug" Morin's fault. Attackmen should never try to keep up with upperclassmen midfielders, whatever the field of play.

I missed most of my junior and senior seasons because of that ankle injury. Otherwise, the Marines might have washed me out and made me miss my chance for an all-expense paid trip to Southeast Asia a year later. I blew out the ankle again in Vietnam while coordinating an emergency extract of a Marine recon team near the Laotian border. Ground fire hits to the cockpit of my OV-10 Bronco spotter plane, while flying at tree top level coordinating the medevacs and close air support, twisted my ankle under the rudder pedals. Who says attackmen aren't lucky, immortal or senseless from taking too many hits to the head crossing in front of the crease?

As we limped our way back to the DaNang Air Base, I was hoping that if we crashed it would be at the south end of the field where the Navy's All-American midfielder and "Topgun" Jimmy Lewis was rumored to be based. I always wanted to get his autograph as the "Greatest Living Lacrosse Player".

Never having played lacrosse before Notre Dame or gotten into a fight before the Marines, I now believe the two had an evolutionary connection, beyond my problematic ankle. Both involvements initially seemed unthinkable and unattainable for a former high school tennis player from a cushy Detroit suburb who dared to think he could play a contact sport at Notre Dame, not to mention going on to serve with a "few good men" in the most unforgiving competition of all.

Credit Notre Dame Lacrosse for getting me out of my comfort zone, making me more physically confident, and giving me the chance to relish the camaraderie of a "band of brothers". Our lacrosse club was led by selfless characters like upperclassmen Matt Dwyer, Len Niessen and John Brandau, along with fearless and certifiable nutballs like Bob "Slug" Morin, Bob "Rabbit" Noonan and Pete "Mouse " Sillari. Noonan later went on to be an Army general, starting with his tour of duty in Vietnam down in the Mekong Delta as an intelligence officer, and Sillari flew combat missions off a carrier in the Gulf of Tonkin.

Even before my Marine training and learning of legendary leaders like Chesty Puller, who inspired his unit while outnumbered and surrounded in Korea in the dead of winter, I met the equally uncompromising and inspiring Jack Tate. Against all odds, he started Notre Dame lacrosse from scratch with little assistance from the university. He quietly and stoically took no prisoners whether it be practicing without enough helmets or convincing all of us lacrosse neophytes that we could learn the game of Indian warriors, regardless of our size and backgrounds. Before I encountered my first

Marine drill instructor, co-captain Matt Dwyer's gravelly voice became indelible. I'll never forget his terrifying orders to his fellow defensemen to pick up any errant attackmen entering their zone and to take them out without mercy. It didn't matter if it was just an intrasquad scrimmage.

As a club sport, Notre Dame Lacrosse also introduced me to the importance of selflessness, shared sacrifice and determination to accomplish the mission, no matter how under resourced or outmanned we were. Consider the sight of five us packed into my four-seater Corvair with an interior exhaust leak for a fifteen hours of tag team driving and resuscitation to get to Annapolis to play Navy's freshman team. Outnumbered 3 to 1, they only beat us in the final period by a goal.

I was not alone in 1969 making the lacrosse and military connection. I felt a special kinship with other teammates like Chuck Metzger, Ford Cole and others who served. At our recent 50th reunion, Chuck and I secretly plotted to raid the equipment room at the new lacrosse stadium in hopes of scoring one of those seemingly gold-plated helmets today's varsity players wear.

Had we been successful, true to Notre Dame Club Lacrosse, we would have celebrated our tactical victory at the closest bar and passed our helmet trophy around to collect enough money to get something to eat. Then we'd be waiting for our re-cycled football jerseys to dry in the laundromat so we would be ready for our next "what though the odds be great or small" challenge as "loyal sons marching onward to victory".

Mike Cerre (left) in Vietnam

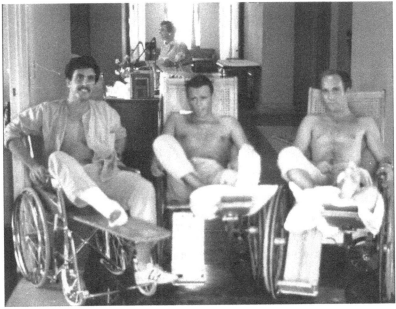

Mike Cerre (left) in Vietnam

Jack Pierce '70

New Englander Jack Pierce entered Notre Dame in 1965. He fought in the Bengal Bouts as a heavyweight, losing in the 1968 finals to footballer Chuck Landolfi. After his Navy career, he played club lacrosse in California, often lining up against former Domers. In 2002, Jack was selected to play and compete in the Lacrosse World Games in Sydney, Australia on the USA Masters Lacrosse Team. In 2014 he was inducted into the USA Lacrosse Hall of Fame, Northern California Chapter.

Club President Instrumental in Keeping Irish Lacrosse Alive

The war in Vietnam was raging in 1966, when I began my freshman year at Notre Dame. Draft boards across the country called up swelling numbers of young men to meet the manpower needs of our military. College students weren't subject to the draft until graduation. But I wanted more control over my destiny, so I joined Navy ROTC.

My freshman year platoon leader was John Lancaster, a senior who would become a Marine after graduation. He received orders to Vietnam and arrived there during the pivotal Tet Offensive of 1968. Five months later, John was shot in the back during a firefight, suffering a spinal injury that left him paralyzed from the waist down. That injury set him off on a remarkable career path that is worth noting because it represents the best of the Notre Dame spirit and character. First, John earned a law degree at Notre Dame, nudging the school toward awareness of the needs of the disabled. His determination to be an advocate and difference-maker led him to a position at the White House, where he worked on the implementation of the Americans with Disabilities Act. Later, as a publication of the United States Institute for Peace notes, John returned to Vietnam, helping to help establish programs for the disabled and spending "nearly five years working in support of men whom war had once defined as his enemies."

During my senior year, Jim Salscheider (ND Captain '65) invited me join him as a member of the Los Angeles Lacrosse Club team. That would have been fun, but I told him I was expecting to receive orders to serve in the Atlantic or Mediterranean. Bad guess. Shortly after I was commissioned in June of 1970, I received orders to report to Amphibious Warfare School at the U.S. Navy SEALS Base in Coronado, California. Following training to land SEALS and Marines on beaches, I was assigned to the USS Juneau LPD-10. Not long after that, we sailed from Long Beach for our first 9-month tour of Vietnam.

My first day-job aboard the ship was as Personnel and Legal Officer. I had a division of about fifteen men who ran the administrative side of shipboard operations. In my "battle job" ("General Quarters"), I was the Boat Group Commander for amphibious assaults. I was the first guy to the beach, the guy in the orange life vest—which seemed like a bullseye to me—whose responsibility was to direct the multiple waves of amphibious craft. The Marines were in floating tanks, LVTs, whose armor protected them. I was in a flimsy fiberglass Captain's gig, standing up to give the signals to direct the traffic.

Nine months later I joined Jim Salscheider as a member of the L.A. Lacrosse Club. Under the excellent tutelage of two Hall of Fame lacrosse defensemen, Bill Shoop and Ray Breslau, I honed my skills as a defenseman and played at a level of lacrosse that was more advanced than what I had experienced as a club player in the Midwest. I played against some of the best in the game, most notably attackman Jimmy Lewis, a Naval Academy grad and a three-time winner of the Turnbull Award, which is awarded to the top attackman at the collegiate level.

Then came another surprise. I never expected I would do a second Vietnam tour. In had been talking with my "detailer" about getting assigned to the East Coast for my next billet. But I had made the mistake of becoming a good ship handler. The Juneau was a 582-foot amphibious ship that carried a crew of 465 Sailors, 800 Marines, 6 helicopters and 25 "Mike" boats. It had a tapered bow and a flat stern. It was a city-block long and difficult to maneuver, especially in tight spaces. Our "skipper" (captain) had designated me as his junior officer ship-handler in competitive training drills for which the ship--and the Skipper--were graded. Then, when I was in Okinawa, expecting orders to my next ship, I was ordered to do a second Vietnam tour on the Juneau. I later found out that the captain had requested this. Such is life.

When my time was up, I turned down the skipper's offer of a "walks-on-water" recommendation for Destroyer School in Newport, Rhode Island. That would have opened the door to a promising Navy career. I thanked him but told him I was heading to law school.

I thought that was the end of my Navy career. And, it was-- until 1995, when I was invited to play on the USNA Navy "Old Goats" Super Masters Team at Vail. Jimmy Lewis was one of my teammates. I am now in my 25th year with that team, still playing the game I love. But that's a story for another time.

Editor's Note: The 1969 season was a challenging one for the ND Lacrosse Club. The abrupt departure of a team leader who left the lacrosse program was a big blow. Against the background of a campus increasingly preoccupied by the war in Vietnam, enthusiasm waned and the team struggled. But our fortunes began to reverse with the post-season election of co-captains Jack Pierce, a Bengal Bouts veteran, and Tim McHugh, whose love of the game, talent for organization and commitment to rigorous conditioning were great for morale.

Another big boost came over the summer when Jack, having finished his Naval ROTC midshipman's cruise in California, flew to Chicago and took the South Shore to South Bend. There the Notre Dame admissions office, in a gesture that today's privacy laws would make impossible, allowed him to examine the files of incoming freshmen. After identifying those who had been varsity athletes in high school, he sent out letters inviting them to participate in an introductory lacrosse clinic early in the upcoming school year.

A few weeks later, on the field next to Stepan Center, several dozen recruits were introduced to the skills of stick-handling, scooping, passing and catching. About 20 would do well enough to stick with the team. Two years later, when Rich O'Leary was in his second year as ND's first lacrosse coach, several of the Pierce recruits played key roles in the team's march to the Midwest Club Championship. One year after that, two of them--Rich Mullin and Dave Jurusik--were elected co-captains for the 1973 team. It is not an exaggeration to say that Jack's recruitment coup was crucial to the club's ability to gather the momentum that carried ND lacrosse to varsity status. -JK

Tim McHugh '70

Tim McHugh served as co-captain of Notre Dame lacrosse, later served in the Coast Guard and had a career in maritime law before his passing in 2018. This tribute is provided by Jerry Kammer.

Two Lax Leaders Meet on the Field at Georgetown

At halftime of the 1970 game at Georgetown, the team was in a hole. The Hoyas, in their first year as a varsity squad, were up, 6-3. But Notre Dame co-captains Tim McHugh and Jack Pierce had a good feeling about the team's chances.

"We were hustling. We had legs," Tim said later. He and Jack knew they had prepared the team well, putting them through a Spartan pre-season training regime that featured not only the customary, grueling sprints to the top steps of the football stadium but also new wrinkle that Pierce and fellow defenseman Chris Servant had brought over from the Bengal Bouts. As Tim later put it with his characteristically dry wit, the two pugilists had led the team through "parts of South Bend and Mishawaka not recently seen by anyone else."

In the second half, ND conditioning began wearing the Hoyas down. The score at the end the third quarter was 6-4. Then another goal made things really tight. After that, things got a little "chippy," especially after what the Irish regarded as a flagrant attempt by a frustrated Hoya to decapitate one of the inexhaustible boys from South Bend. Tim, incredulous that the assault drew no whistle from the referee, had just begun to protest when, to everyone's astonishment, a husky blonde-haired guy leaped from the stands and sprinted onto the field to inform the negligent ref that he was definitely a homer and probably an idiot.

Tim, preferring to have the ref to himself, turned to the intruder with an inquiry as to what the hell he was doing. He received a response that he later described in writing: "Big smile, eyes crinkled behind horn rims. 'Oh, hi, Tim. I'm Jack Tate.' Then he turned to his teammates and explained, "That was our Founding Father."

It was a surreal moment in a game that proceeded to an nail-biting conclusion. With a little more than a minute on the clock, Tim sent a shot high and hard past the Hoya goalie, knotting the score at 6-6 and sending the game to overtime, which Ken Lund ended with an equally dramatic goal. That triggered a celebration that carried over to the locker room when some ND fans delivered champagne.

It was an unforgettable game that was a peak moment for the unforgettable Timothy Reardon McHugh. Tim was intense in so many ways, sometimes to the point of ferocity. He was intense in his intelligence, his sarcasm, his commitment to the team. That mid-game encounter with the equally intense Jack Tate was a meeting of two irrepressible guys who were indispensable to the evolution of Notre Dame lacrosse from club to varsity status.

A year earlier, in the early spring of 1969, the club had come close to unraveling after our captain had abruptly left school to deal with a personal emergency that occupied him for weeks. The fragile organizational framework that was inherent in club status—putting the captain in charge of off-the-field administration as well as on-the-field strategy—was obliterated. This came against the background of a campus roiled by protests against the Vietnam War that had become so tense that in February Father Hesburgh made national news with his stern 15-minute rule against protests that disrupted university operations. It was on multiple levels a season of discontent.

In partnership with Jack Pierce, another alpha-male with a fierce desire to build a successful team, Tim McHugh provided the stabilizing force that held the team together and tightened our brotherhood. Their off-season planning and recruitment set the stage for 1970 to become a time of rebuilding, especially with the athletes Jack recruited with his letter-writing campaign to incoming freshman who had been successful athletes in high school. That group would be the nucleus of the team that became Midwestern Club champions in 1972 and would go on to the best club record of 10-1 in 1973.

Tim McHugh remains vivid in the memories of those who knew him. "He brewed a wonderful camaraderie," said Ed Hoban. "He got us ready to play the game." Jim Laffey, whom Tim recruited at the 1967 Club Night that introduced incoming freshman to extracurricular possibilities, recalled that Tim "gave me the feeling that the team would be both competitive and fun." Tim's younger brother Tom recalled that in early visits to campus, when he hung out with Tim, "I was drawn by the camaraderie, the friendships. I wanted to be a part of it. "

Tim's attraction to South Bend was shaped by a generational pull that emanated from three maternal uncles who had attended ND. In 1966 he graduated from Portsmouth Priory, a Catholic school in Rhode Island, close to the sea that had shaped what Tom called their father's "inherited dominant trait." James F. McHugh was a Navy commander during World War II. For much of the rest of his life he was involved in efforts to conserve marine habitat and resources. He was an adviser to the U.S. delegation to the International Commission for the Conservation of Atlantic Tuna. He served on the Mid-Atlantic Fisheries Management Council and was active in several efforts to protect the Chesapeake Bay.

With that genetic inheritance, Tim was drawn to the Coast Guard. Within a year of graduation he had completed Officer Candidate School and was an officer aboard the cutter Vigilant. Home port was New Bedford, Mass, where Jack Pierce's future wife, Julie Bernas, was in grad school. Julie and Tim became good friends. Her fond memory of a visit to the Vigilant is a classic tale about the intense Mr. McHugh. Julie said that at fine dinner aboard the ship, "I learned more about the LORAN navigation system than I ever thought I needed to know!"

After serving on the Vigilant, Tim was assigned as a staff officer, first in Boston and then in Washington. He worked on fisheries regulations and participated in negotiations with the governments of Russia, Norway and other countries on issues of maritime regulation and safety. He also served as a liaison officer with the Congress and federal agencies.

Tim was a busy man in Washington. He married, started a family and earned a law degree through an evening program at American University. That led to a long career in maritime law in Boston and Southborough, Mass. He coached youth soccer and lacrosse and did other volunteer work. Says daughter Emily," He knew and loved every inch of Southborough."

Emily talks fondly of the lessons she learned from her father. "He taught me you have a course to steer, no matter what the adversity," she said. He told her about the Coast Guard motto, "Semper paratus'—Always prepared. Emily applied that lesson to soccer. "I learned you've got to practice. You've got to stay focused." She became captain of her high school team.

Emily was moved by the way he dealt with the early-onset Alzheimer's that forced him to leave his law practice in 2008. "It strips away a lot of the stress," she said. The most challenging thing to see was also the most beautiful thing to see. His true nature shone through. I got to know my dad without all the pressures of ordinary life. He was the funniest, most loving, most giving guy."

In March of 2018, Tim McHugh died of complications of Alzheimer's, a cruelly ironic malady for a man of his brilliant intensity. Dave Jurusik, who as a freshman recorded his first goal in that 1970 Georgetown game, spoke for the entire team when he wrote of his admiration for Co-Captains

McHugh and Pierce: "They were tough, disciplined leaders, and our pre-season workouts were gruesome. They taught us to be tough, relentless, and enduring. They helped forge our characters, and they taught us teamwork. I am forever grateful for being part of the ND Lacrosse Brotherhood."

USCGC Vigilant (WMEC-617)

Chris Servant '70

Chris Servant came to Notre Dame from Attleboro Falls, Massachusetts in 1966. He fought in the Bengal Bouts and was the middleweight champ in 1968 and 1969. Chris played defense on the lacrosse team and graduated with a BA in English. He served in US Navy in Vietnam. Chris had a long career in education and was the winner of the Alumni Association's Reynolds Award.

Defenseman and Bengal Bouter Served in Vietnam

My decision to attend Notre Dame was based on the recommendation of my brother Greg (ND '69). I had never visited or seen the campus.

I left my home in Massachusetts with an uncle who drove my brother and me there and dropped us off. Little did I know that I would not return home for 117 days. That first year was filled with a great deal of work, little social life, and even less activity.

As a sophomore, I declared English as a major, got to select a better room in Alumni Hall, solidified my freshmen friendships, tutored junior high kids, boxed in the Bengal Bouts and vastly improved my grades. Life was good.

That spring, a Massachusetts friend, Jack Pierce, talked me into playing club lacrosse. I knew nothing about the game, and like most beginners, struggled to "cradle," "scoop," and "pass," but it was fun.

As a junior, I played in the fall program, and my skills improved enough to get "invited" to go on the spring trip to Colorado. (Are you familiar with" Drive-Aways"?) I believe we played Air Force and Denver. I don't think we won either game.

The most enduring memory of the Colorado trip was having to hitchhike 1,500 miles back to South Bend with teammate Jack Pierce. After standing in 30-degree temperatures most of the night, we finally got a lift from a guy driving a truck load of cattle to the Chicago stock yards. (think John Candy in "Trains, Planes and Automobiles").

After 36 hours on the road, we arrived in South Bend at 7 a.m.... and had to play Bowling Green at 10. We got hammered 15-2.

That spring, I played my best game against Ohio University, which we won 5-2. Unfortunately, I broke my left hand in the game, and felt my season was over, until I met a resourceful orthpod at St. Joe's Hospital who agreed to cast my hand while holding a broom stick.

As senior, I got to start on defense, but we struggled to win, despite a top goalie (Jerry Kammer '71), a prolific scorer (Ken Lund '71), solid midfielders (the Bingle brothers '69,'70), and a superb player/coach (Tim McHugh '70). Our spring trip took us East to the DC area where we played and beat Mount St. Mary's (8-6) and upset Georgetown (7-6) in their first-ever varsity game.

I entered the Navy through the NROTC program, which I had joined as a sophomore. After my graduation and commissioning on June 4th, 1970, I reported for duty to the Richard B, Anderson DD-786 in San Diego. There, I attended ASROC school to become the ship's Anti-Submarine ROcket Controller. Then I left for Vietnam.

I was the ship's First Lieutenant. We did a great deal of plane guarding for the carriers and provided gun-fire support for Marines and SEAL team guys on the beach. No sooner did we finish that first West PAC tour than we embarked on a second deployment.

I recall riding out a typhoon in the Gulf of Tonkin and experiencing 45-degree rolls. We became the first American ship to be fired upon at Phu Quoc Island, off the coast of Cambodia.

The Navy was withdrawing from Vietnam and offered 50,000 "reserve" officers an "early out." I had already been accepted to ND Law School. I took the offer and drove directly to South Bend, only to be informed by Dean Broderick that law school classes had started two weeks earlier!

I returned home. While waiting for the second semester to start in January, I started teaching English at my alma mater, Bishop Feehan. I began to realize that my passion was teaching and working with high school students. In December, I was offered a full-time job teaching English and coaching football. Forty-four years later, in 2016, I retired as the school's first President. As a result of my work at Feehan. I was honored to receive the Notre Dame Alumni

Association's *2019 William D, Reynolds Award*, for *"improving the lives and the education of youth."*

I have been married for 47 years, have four married children, (41, 39, 37 and 35.) who have blessed my wife and me, with ten grandchildren. Over the years, I have been able to attend my reunions and see a few football games. But a personal highlight for me, as attending the 2014 National Lacrosse Championships (Baltimore) when Duke beat ND 11-9. I was moved that there was a special recognition made of the past ND lacrosse players, especially the first ones, who sustained the growth of the program while playing club lacrosse.

Fred Bingle '70

Fred Bingle, from Toledo, Ohio was the first of four Bingle Brothers to play lacrosse at ND. Fred graduated with a Business degree in 1970 and served in the Army Reserves for six years. He obtained an MBA from Ohio State and works in Market Research.

Midfielder Leads Band of Bingles to Irish Lacrosse

Being a member of the Notre Dame lacrosse team was the best part of Notre Dame and, really, one of the best times of my lifetime. I made a lot of great friends and had some fun times and it got me involved in lacrosse – the best sport ever.

I came to Notre Dame in fall of 1966 from Toledo, Ohio. My brother, Bill was a junior then and I followed him to the Dome. Funny, but it ended up that all five of the Bingle boys made it to ND and graduated and four of us, Jimmy (Middie), BJ (Attack), Tommy (Attack) and me (Middie) played on the lacrosse team. Not many can say that. And play got better with the younger brothers.

In the fall of freshman year, there was a sports or activity call out at Stepan Center. I had played sports in high school and wanted to do something at ND on the club level. There was soccer, rugby, crew. Then I saw the lacrosse table. I had never heard of lacrosse but thought it looked like fun. You got to use a stick and it was a combination of the skills of several sports. I decided to give it a try and was glad I did.

Freshman year was tough, just learning to pass, catch, cradle and pick-up ground balls, in addition to playing defense and enduring the workouts and practices. The cold workouts under the stadium and running the steps, jumping jacks and playing games in snow and cold weather. A funny story is that freshman year, in the last practice before spring break, Pete Metzger was coming down on a fast break and I hit him with my fists on his shoulder and snapped my right wrist. I didn't know it then, but I found out it was broken in the summer and then I wore a cast all summer and even into the fall season, taping my lax gloves around the cast and playing on.

There were lots of good friends, like Tim McHugh, Jack Pierce, Chris Servant, Freddy Morrison, Kenny Lund, Jerry Kammer and guys on the team I met through Jimmy and BJ.

I have a couple of funny stories from when I ran the Boston Marathon my senior year. I had no idea how far that was and figured I could always jog. Boy, was I wrong. However, I did finish it, running in my ND lacrosse shirt and my Johnny Dee low cuts (knock offs of Converse All Stars). I couldn't walk for a week and McHugh was pissed. But that was partly just Tim being Tim.

Then another time, senior year, our game against Ohio U was cancelled and we decided to go to D.C. for an anti-war rally. Kenny Lund, me, Tommy Nelesen and I'm not sure who else hopped in the "Prince" (my old Plymouth Valiant) and headed to D.C. to stay at Nelesen's sister's apartment. It was a fun trip, but I cut my heel in the reflecting pool by the Lincoln Monument. I had trouble playing for a week again. It was a rough senior year.

We had fun game trips over spring break. The Kammer house in Baltimore was base camp, and we won our games against Georgetown and Mount St. Mary's. Then down to Denison. I remember we were up 1-0 on Denison, one of the top Midwest teams at the time, but then lost by double digits.

Senior year, we also had the "Laffey Sandwich" midfield line. Jim Laffey was in the middle, between my brother, Jimmy and me. Poor Laffey, but we had fun.

I enjoyed my "playing days" at ND and after school ended up playing on club teams in Columbus and Indianapolis. I also coached the U. of Toledo team for a couple years. Later on, I got involved with girls' youth lacrosse with my daughter and started and coached a girls' youth team in Indianapolis, the Saints. I also assisted with her high school team. Lacrosse has been a good long-term involvement.

For the military, I served in the U.S. Army Reserves from 1970-1976. I was lucky to get in the Reserves rather than being drafted. We had come back to ND from Christmas break in January 1970 to the first Vietnam War draft lottery. My number was 52, so there was a good chance of getting drafted. There was a Reserve unit in my hometown, Toledo, and I applied and was accepted. My dad had been in the Army in World War II in the Pacific battle area. My older brother, Bill, had been in Air Force ROTC and after law school he went into the Air Force at the Northern Michigan base.

I did my basic and AIT at Ft. Leonard Wood in Missouri. Boy, I hated that place and was glad to leave. I was in a Reserve engineering unit, and we also had a quarry unit and road paving unit. My MOS (military occupational specialty) was as a Quarry machine operator (Rock crusher). So, when we went to summer camp, I worked in the quarry, making small rocks out of big rocks. Our paving unit and quarry units went together. But sometimes, we would go to a different camp than our headquarters because they needed roads paved. This usually turned out well as we would be assigned to another unit and they left us alone because they needed a certain number of road miles paved for the summer. Our unit was the best and very productive. Our summer camps were at Camp Drum in upstate New York, Camp McCoy in Wisconsin and one in Virginia. Usually a good two weeks, but I was glad when they were done.

Compared to others at this time, my service time was pretty uneventful since I didn't get assigned to Vietnam or serve in Europe or Alaska. But, in 1976, my six years were up, I got out and didn't re-up for any more service time. However, being a veteran has helped me later in life because I'm eligible to use the great VA hospital in Indianapolis. And it has helped my consulting career somewhat.

While still in the Reserves, I obtained an MBA at *The* Ohio State University and got into the market research field. I have been in Indianapolis since around 1983 and may now officially be a Hoosier. I have had my own market research consulting firm since 2000. I am still working away and busier than ever. I enjoy what I do helping clients. I am married to my wonderful wife, Lillian and have two daughters, Hilary who lives in Chicago and Annie who is a junior at Purdue and my lacrosse player. Unfortunately, my wife and older daughter are Purdue grads and my youngest is a junior. I'm surrounded by Boilers.

As a quick update to those who knew me and my brothers: Bill is an attorney in Toledo. Jimmy is a cardiologist in Toledo. BJ is an attorney in Chicago. And Tommy is the lead person at an alumni travel company in Chicago but lives in Boston. All are doing well and we still stay in touch through Zoom meetings, our annual Brothers' weekend in Michigan, and our kids' weddings.

Thank you to Len and all our lacrosse brothers for this chance to share stories and enhance the fellowship our ND lax community.

Go Irish!

Kenny Lund '71

Kenny Lund entered ND in 1967 and was destined to become one of the club's leading point getters, finishing in the top ten in goals, assists and points (43/23/66). Ken graduated with a liberal arts degree and spent 20 years in the Army before retiring as a major.

High Scoring Attackman Becomes Screaming Eagle

The first complete lacrosse game I attended was one I played in. Having graduated from a small high school in southern Missouri, and grown up in a military family as the son of an Army sergeant stationed nowhere near the East Coast, lacrosse was a complete unknown when I arrived at Notre Dame in the fall of 1967. It would probably have remained that way had it not been for Hugh DePaolo, a fellow Zahmbie and a fencer, who was tossing the ball around in front of the dorm with another fellow as I was returning from class one day. The sticks, of course, were of the wood, leather and cat gut variety, and after a few toss abouts I accepted Hugh's invitation to show up for a practice at the north end of the stadium. I was enthusiastically welcomed by Tim McHugh and was given a stick the size of a garden rake to use for the passing and scoop drills. I remember being impressed, and somewhat intimidated by the skill, athletic ability and enthusiasm of the players on the team. More importantly their passion for the game, camaraderie, and friendship made me want to be a part of the Notre Dame Lacrosse experience, a brotherhood I still feel a part of over fifty years later.

Playing in the early part of the "hybrid era" '67 to '71 included fall practices in the stadium, running the stairs, drills and sprints under the stands, and selling programs at home football games. At some point, I think the early spring, we moved to the old field house after the basketball floor was removed and worked out. We had the wooden shed which housed our equipment, and it proved to be a decent place to run practices. More than a few times Coach Parseghian or one of his minions would come down to say "Wrap it up, boys...the team's coming in" as the football players arrived for spring practice. We were allowed to use nicer facilities after the ACC was opened.

Away games were always an adventure, travelling to schools in whatever vehicles the upperclassmen on the team owned at the time, and never being sure where we were staying until we got there. The bulk of my trips were made in the back of a Plymouth Valiant (the Prince), owned by Freddy Bingle. Senior year I rocketed across the Midwest in a Shelby Cobra owned and operated by Ed Hoban who set several land speed records between South Bend and the Ohio state line.

My world changed dramatically at the start of my junior year, when I married the love of my life Marti. That meant my junior and senior year I was married, had a son, Christopher, worked a job at the ND ticket office, tried to finish school, complete ROTC requirements and play lacrosse. Looking back, I know that the things that kept me going were my wonderful wife, the ND lacrosse experience and the friendship and support I received from my teammates.

One of the things that kept me sane was actually the insanity of the lacrosse parties we used to have at various off campus locations. Most were epic events filled with music, noise, singing, belly bouncing and other activities so profound and disgusting that decorum prohibits listing them here.

Among the many highlights two stand out: the singing of "Runaround Sue" by Dion and the Belmonts, led by yours truly and enthusiastically backed up by the whole team, and an infamous skit known as "Stick a Feather Up Your A** ", directed by Ed Hoban. The former was not only sung masterfully by the attendees but also choreographed. The latter became an initiation ritual that had to be performed by the freshmen and any newcomers to the team at the first party of the season. I am thankful there was no social media available at the time.

On the day before graduating from Our Lady's University I was commissioned as a second lieutenant in the United States Army. Upon completion of the Field Artillery Officer's Basic Course at Ft. Sill, Oklahoma I was assigned to Germany, where my family and I ended up staying for four years. I held a number of duty assignments while there, my first one was in an Honest John rocket battalion. The Honest John was a long range, truck mounted artillery rocket capable of both an atomic or high explosive warhead. It was the first US tactical nuclear weapon. I also served as the executive officer of an 8 inch howitzer battery, and as an assistant personnel officer for the 72nd Field Artillery Group, where I also taught race relations. Since all of the combat units in Europe at the time served as "the tip of the spear" in the ongoing Cold War with Russia and its allies, these units spent an inordinate amount of time training in several sites situated along the Czechoslovakian border, sometimes in excess of 150 days a year.

The good news is, when I was not in the field my wife Marti and I travelled to England, Belgium, France, Spain, Copenhagen, Italy and Austria in addition to numerous locations in Germany. Only two friends came to visit and travel with us while we were in Europe...both were lacrosse teammates. Jerry Kammer and Kent "Hilde" Hildebrand visited and spent time with us while we were there.

Upon returning to the States in 1975 I was assigned to the famous 101st Airborne Division (Air Assault) at Ft. Campbell, Kentucky. While serving with the Screaming Eagles, I held positions as an assistant battalion operations officer, an infantry battalion fire support officer in a unit commanded by then COL Colin Powell, and had the privilege to command C Battery, 1/321 Field Artillery. As a rapid deployment force the 101st had a variety of missions, all of which we trained for including large scale exercises with the 82nd Airborne and a three week deployment to the Jungle Operations Training Center in Panama. One of the best things about being at Ft. Campbell was that it was within driving distance to South Bend for the annual Lacrosse alumni games, which I was finally able to attend.

After a short stop at the Armored Officer Advanced Course at Ft. Knox, we moved to the Washington D.C. area, where I served in a branch of the Pentagon known as the Military Personnel Center, holding down several positions dealing with Officer Personnel Management, or Manglement depending on who you talked to. The huge advantage of this move was that I once again was able to pick up a lacrosse stick and play with the Alexandria Lacrosse Club, an organization founded by Notre Dame lacrosse alumnus Tom McHugh, the younger brother of Tim. Other ex-ND stickmen on the team included Jimmy Brown, Dave Jurusik, and Joe Anderson.

After D.C. I moved the family to Ft. Richardson, Alaska situated just outside of Anchorage for an assignment to the 172nd Light Infantry Brigade, the "Home of the Arctic Soldier." There I served as operations officer for the 1/37th Field Artillery Battalion, brigade fire support officer, and infantry brigade S-1, or personnel officer. As an arctic infantry brigade most of our field exercises were conducted during the winter months, many of them at Ft. Greely, where the average daily temperature could be minus 10 degrees. We often operated at minus twenty and joked that the only thing that worked at minus twenty was a soldier. Cold weather survival was always the first mission. The last day I spent in the field I operated a landing zone at Ft. Greely. The wind chill index was around minus 42 degrees but seemed to drop to about 212 degrees under the helicopter rotors.

On the other hand, summers in The Great Land were glorious: 24 hours of sunlight, abundant open space to explore and camp in and plentiful waters to fish. My two sons absolutely loved living there and left kicking and screaming for our next duty station in Denver, Colorado where I worked as an advisor to the U. S. Army Reserve and National Guard units in a four-state area including Colorado, Wyoming, North Dakota and South Dakota. My team consisted of personnel from the combat arms specialties, matching the types of units each state had in their organizations. The last major mission I was involved in was the training and certification of units called up for service in Operation Desert Storm. I retired from the Army in May of 1991, after 20 years of active duty. It was my great honor and privilege to serve this great nation of ours.

I am fond of saying that people go to Notre Dame for many reasons: because their parents went there, to prepare for a certain career, or to get into an elite grad school. Those are but a few incentives to walk the hallowed ground of Our Lady's University. I used to say I attended ND for one reason and one reason only: to meet my wife Marti. I now realize that there was another important reason I ended up there. So that fifty years down the road I could still have and enjoy the company of dear friends that I bonded with playing Notre Dame lacrosse.

172nd Light Infantry Brigade (Arctic) Ft. Greely AK, 1985

Rich O'Leary- Coach

Rich O'Leary played high school lacrosse at East Meadow High on Long Island and continued playing at Nassau Community College and Cortland State. His outstanding career at Cortland was capped by his being named to the North-South all-star game played in Lexington, KY. He was an assistant lacrosse coach at Cornell when he was hired for the ND job. Rich lost his battle with cancer in 2009 but not before he had left his mark not only on the ND lacrosse program but on the many men who played for Rich and looked at him as a surrogate father. This remembrance of Rich comes from Dave Jurusik..

The Luck of the IRISH

Some folks would say Moose Krause was one of the founders of ND Lacrosse, though his name rarely comes up when discussing the early years of the ND Lacrosse program. But Moose Krause was responsible for hiring Rich O'Leary to be the Assistant Director of Intramural Sports and the coach of the ND Lacrosse Club. We have no idea how many folks submitted resumes for the position, how many were interviewed, nor who the final candidates were for the position. But we do know Moose Krause made the right decision in hiring Rich O'Leary.

Rich played his college lacrosse at SUNY Cortland where he was a two-time All-American attackman. He was a good athlete and we all appreciated and respected that about our new coach. Rich knew we were athletes who loved competition and had a disdain for losing. He knew we had limited lacrosse experience, but he respected our athletic abilities and our willingness to work hard to learn the skills to be good lacrosse players.

Jim Lepley '73 recalled, "Right after we met Rich our sophomore year, he invited several of us for dinner at his home, which at that time was a manufactured house (mobile home). We met Linda who cooked a great spaghetti dinner for us. We all fell in love with Linda that evening."

Rich didn't coach with a heavy hand, barking commands like a drill sergeant or yelling when we made mistakes. He didn't waste any breath chastising us for dropping passes or making a bad throw to a teammate. Rich was the most patient soul on the field when it came to our practices. He coached us by encouraging us to constantly work on the fundamentals of passing and catching. He explained the movement of the ball and play on the field in terms we could relate to from our knowledge of hockey, soccer and basketball, sports that many of us had played in high school.

Ed Hoban '72, co-captain of the 1972 ND Lacrosse Club, has fond memories of Rich. "I remember countless overnights at Rich and Linda's home in the Bend," Ed said. "They welcomed us into their family early on. I remember chasing their kids around the house as the Tickle Machine. Playing with Rich for

Chicago Lacrosse club was a special treat. It was obvious he was an All-American for a reason. He was totally unselfish on the field and so much fun off the field. When he arrived, Notre Dame Lacrosse began. Not to discount the player/coaches that came before him. They were legendary in their own right, great players and lots of fun. But when I think of Rich, I think of a man with love, humility, and a sense of humor. A cynic without being mean. He was gifted! Long live Rich O'Leary!"

Gary Riopko '72, who was co-captain along with Ed Hoban in 1972 remembers one of the famous "Richisms" to this day. *Get your playing time in when you are on the field.* "My daughter and I have been coaching young girls' teams for six years and we tell that to them at every practice. They are as confused with it as we were. We all played for the love of the game, and that's probably why Rich made Notre Dame his home."

Rich "Moons" Mullin '73, who co-captained the 1973 team with me, remained in South Bend after graduation and kept in close contact with Coach. Moons mentioned, "What amazed me after spending time with Rich after graduation, was that he not only had a loyal following of ND players that he coached, but he was loved and appreciated by hundreds of students in his role as Assistant Director of non-varsity sports. Further, nearly everyone working on campus knew Rich. He also helped maintain the support of the alumni players by reaching out to men like John "Tuna" Driscoll and Jack Tate, and hosting the Friday night get-together at his house on Alumni weekend. At the end of our junior year after we won the Midwest Club Lacrosse title, Rich told me, Dave and some of the returning seniors that Moose Krause had some thoughts of taking the club to varsity status. But Rich was quick to inform us that all it really meant was very little financial support and many NCAA regulations! We were glad to remain a club our senior year."

Jim Lepley '73 recalled, "For Rich's birthday our senior year, when we had a 10-1 record, we all pitched in and bought him a 10-speed Schwinn bicycle, which Rich later told us he had for many years. There was something unique about Rich's character and demeanor that really brought out the best in us as competitors and made us feel proud that we played for him and for ND!"

Jim Brown '73, a teammate of Jim Lepley's, remembers Rich was a man of few words. "My senior year we were playing the Columbus Lacrosse Club in Columbus. We had a good team and were undefeated. The game was close and the Columbus goalie was hot. At some point in the game, much to my surprise, I found myself on a breakaway, just me and the goalie! I shot, hit the goalie squarely in the middle of his chest! When the lines changed and I got back to the bench, Rich looked at me and said "Brownie, you've got to aim the ball!" Yeah Coach, I get it. I learned that day to not just shoot, but shoot with aim and purpose. Rich was a man of few words, but when he spoke, we all listened. He was a great guy and a great coach!"

Jim Scarola '78, captain of the team and a converted goalie playing attackman his senior year, had this memorable comment about Rich. "I learned from Rich that great leaders are not defined by titles or positions they have held, but rather by the impact they have had on the people around them."

Mike Lynch '82, a member of the group of players who experienced the Club's transition to varsity had this endearing comment. "Rich is what my dad used to call a gentleman's gentleman. A guy you look up to. A guy you want to have a beer with and tell a joke to. A guy with a huge heart, a pure sense of humor and a ton of class. Quite simply, I love the guy."

We band of Notre Dame Lacrosse Brothers who played under Coach Rich O'Leary were truly lucky he got the job. He was the perfect man for the job. And he will never be forgotten by the men who played for him. We know we were blessed with the "Luck of the IRISH."

Captains Rich Mullin and Dave Jurusik with Coach O'Leary

Rich and Linda O'Leary

Sandy Cochran – Coach '72-'76

A Yale graduate, US Army Captain Sandy Cochran served two Vietnam tours and then came to Notre Dame as an ROTC instructor in 1972. He coached the ND lacrosse B team and officiated at the teams' home games. Sandy earned an MS and a PhD in history from Kansas U. He continued to officiate lacrosse but also held a professorship at New Mexico U and served as Historical Advisor to the Army Chief of Staff. Sandy lives in the DC suburbs

Coach and ROTC Instructor Served Two Tours in Vietnam

I grew up in Baltimore, "playing" high school lacrosse. It was all wooden sticks with rawhide "pockets"; I would walk home pounding at that "pocket" but it never seemed to last. Almost all my friends played lacrosse, and so did I, but not very well. I played defense to avoid catching and throwing. I went to Yale and realized that Big Time lacrosse interfered with my drinking and girls... I left my old stick at home.

I joined Army ROTC at Yale as had my role model, my uncle, majoring in history as did he. I graduated in 1961 with John Kennedy's words ringing in my head "ask not what your country can do for you but what you can do for your country". I was designated a distinguished military graduate, thus gaining both a Regular Army Commission (like West Point) in the infantry and also an assignment to Germany at the peak of the Cold War. I spent most of the next three-plus years focused on the "bad guys" (the Soviets). In retrospect, I completely missed the Civil Rights movement at home.

In 1965, I returned to the States as a captain. I was settling in with my new family when I got a call: "We have your orders to Vietnam." I was ordered to report a few weeks later. I went with no special training since it was assumed that I had done all those things that a captain needed to do in Germany. I ended up as a senior advisor to a Vietnam infantry battalion (along with a LT and two NCO's) based in the Mekong Delta, south of Saigon. The most valued lesson I learned (besides staying alive in combat) was if you don't know what to do, just DO IT. I came home to San Diego (my wife's hometown) and thought seriously about resigning my commission. Instead I got orders to go back to Vietnam, where I was again stationed south of Saigon, this time with US troops. I began to see that what the United States was trying to do was to make the Vietnamese army and the country itself look like the US. The more I worked (just like pounding that ball into my stick), the more I realized that this was not the way to do it. As a reward for two Vietnam tours, the Army decided to send me to graduate school. Since I had majored in history at Yale, I elected to take an MA in that subject at the University of Kansas.

As the Vietnam War ground down, I faced a two-year obligation. It was totally unexpected that as an Army major I would be assigned to the Fighting Irish. I learned that Notre Dame insisted that incoming ROTC "faculty" had to have a graduate degree, and Notre Dame had decided to admit women (Yale had been admitting women for almost a decade). The three service departments were placed directly under the Provost Office to keep them under the spotlight for visibility, as were scholarship options. Little did I realize that my die for the next decade was cast by Notre Dame criteria.

The head of the Army unit suggested that although I was meeting the teaching requirement, I work with students in non-academic programs. In this context, I decided to try my sport one more time. Little did I know that the sport was changing, with plastic heads and aluminum handles – not as brutal and faster. The game's tactics had evolved in tandem with the gear. Now there was less emphasis on hitting people and more on working the ball around with quick passes.

I went to see Rich O'Leary, who was in charge of the Club Sports, about playing as Notre Dame faculty. He lent me an old defense stick with webbing, and I started "running around". The highlight came during a fall season half-field scrimmage. I was assigned to crease defense, with the job of guarding Rich. But after I demonstrated that I couldn't stay with him at all, Rich suggested that I could coach the B team. It made sense to me!

From 1972-1976 under Richie's tutelage, I learned more about the new sport. During that time I worked with those who had never played lacrosse and recruited ROTC students who went on to serve on active duty in the final tough years in Vietnam. I worked the sidelines for Richie during varsity games, mostly "running" midfield substitutions. I learned from him that the key to coaching a team sport paralleled military leadership techniques- quizzing players as they came off the field on what they had learned.

A major challenge for the sport was a shortage of officials at both A and B games. Richie pushed me to be the "Notre Dame at Home" official. My work with the lax program got to the Provost Office and Freshman Year. I extended my ROTC assignment for a year making a deal with my wife to resign my commission. I had several offers to stay at Notre Dame, but lacking a PhD made teaching history in the classroom impossible. I realized that coaching was another form of teaching.

Returning to KU for a history PhD, I worked part time coaching and officiating, more of the latter as it proved to be not as time consuming. I continued to run into the great young men I coached at South Bend as it led to more officiating in VA, MD, AL, GA, NC, CA, TX and other areas. I was cleared to work top level high school games as well as NCAA Level II (but never made TV coverage).

Yale's motto was "for God, Country and for Yale", in South Bend it was for "God, Country and Notre Dame" followed by a brisk "sticks up". The discipline of ND taught me much. I always remembered Father Hesburgh's 15-minute rule.

I would never have been able to take a new direction with confidence had I not agreed to go one-on-one with Richie in the fall of 1972 and been trusted to coach the B team! "Sticks Up".

Oh, by the way, after the PhD I spent another 30 years teaching as a civilian… and officiating lacrosse.

Sandy Cochran and his South Vietnamese Counterpart, 1966

Coach Sandy Cochran (far right), 1975

John Moran '73

John Moran came to ND from lacrosse hotbed Long Island in 1969. A middie, John tallied a goal and an assist in his career. He served in the Navy Seebees for 27 years, retiring as a Captain.

From Long Island to Navy Construction Battalion

If it wasn't for lacrosse, I wouldn't have chosen ND. The four "must haves" I was looking for in a college were Navy ROTC, civil engineering, architecture, and lacrosse. I grew up on Long Island and played on a championship lacrosse team at Massapequa High. Most of the team went on to play in college, and I was being recruited by several East Coast schools. At a dinner with all the Long Island kids he was recruiting, Ned Harkness, Cornell's hockey and lacrosse coach, guaranteed us that if we came to Cornell, we'd win a national championship (he was right). Meanwhile, my driver's ed teacher, who had been an All American at Maryland, told me Notre Dame had "an animal lacrosse club". I didn't really care what caliber of team I played on, as long as I could play lacrosse, and ended up casting my lot with the animals.

The team was comprised of a great bunch of guys and some great characters. Freshman memories include winter runs in the snow, stadium steps, "Jack and Julie" leg lifts, and other maniacal conditioning drills. As I recall, Ed Hoban and I were the only freshmen who had played in high school. For our 1969 spring trip, 17 of us drove overnight to Denver in four cars. I was with upperclassmen Jim Wachtel and Navy ROTC "sea daddies" Jack Pierce and Chris Servant. I think we had seven middies, five defensemen, four attack, and goalie Jerry Kammer. The Air Force Academy ran four midfields and we got a little gassed playing at altitude. We then lost an overtime game to Denver. We fared better back in the Midwest and won a few games. It was instilled in me by upperclassmen that we may not win all the games, but we do win all the parties.

That spring, the club got information from the Admissions Office, and wrote invitation letters to all incoming freshmen from Long Island, upstate New York, Baltimore, and East Coast prep schools who were varsity letter winners in any sport. In the fall, we had a great turnout of freshmen, most of whom had never played lacrosse before, but were good athletes and willing to learn. I ended up having the privilege of coaching all that raw talent. I had recurring knee problems from an injury sustained in a B game the previous spring, and had surgery scheduled for spring break of my sophomore year. I sat out the season and coached the fundamentals of scooping in the snow and line drills in the mud to what turned out to be the talented ND Lacrosse Class of '73.

The next year, the team began to blossom under the tutelage of Coach Rich O'Leary. Who could forget his exhortation to "Get your playing time in on the field". We had a winning record, the roster and skill level continued to grow, and I could tell that ND lacrosse had a bright future.

I spent the following year studying architecture in Rome. When I returned for my 5th year, I moved in with Rich Mullin, Dave Jurusik, Jim Lepley and Joe Anderson into what turned out to be the "lacrosse house" for many years. I had the ground floor master bedroom. The only setback was waking up on Saturday mornings before team parties by kegs being rolled through my bedroom to be put on ice in the bathtub. I sat out most of my 5th year until I finished presenting my architecture thesis project, and only played the last few weeks of the season. However, I did make it to all the parties.

I was commissioned in the Navy Civil Engineer Corps and spent 27 years doing shore facilities and infrastructure management. I had multiple stateside and overseas tours in public works, construction and services contracting, and expeditionary construction with the Seabees. I met my wife Janice, a beautiful Navy Nurse, at my first duty station, Patuxent River, MD, and married her four years later. I was deployed for the first year of our marriage, but we got orders together in 1978 and were able to be colocated for the rest of our Navy careers. Patrick, Colleen and Kathleen were born in Philadelphia, Guam and Portsmouth, VA.

I spent a lot of time on islands. My second assignment was as Public Works Officer at a small facility on Grand Turk in the Turks and Caicos Islands. I went from there to a Seabee battalion homeported in Gulfport, MS, and deployed as a construction company commander to Okinawa and then to Diego Garcia, an atoll in the Indian Ocean. During my first tour on Guam, I oversaw planning and operations for construction battalions deployed to Guam and Okinawa, and their detachments in the Philippines and Japan. Then, I ran the U.S. Military's Civic Action program in Micronesia supporting Army, Navy and Air Force Civic Action Teams on Palau, Yap, Truk, Ponape and Kosrae. Later staff assignments involved business trips to Iceland, the Azores, Puerto Rico and Australia (OK. Australia's really a continent, not an island, but I threw it in because the Aussies are so much damned fun). Our second tour on Guam required lots of business trips to Hawaii, and afforded the opportunity for vacation travel with Jan and the kids to Bali, Hong Kong and Japan.

After my first six years in the Navy, I was able to resume playing lacrosse at several duty stations. I played for the Berkeley Lacrosse Club for two years while I lived in Oakland. We played against Jack Pierce and the San Francisco Lacrosse Club each season. I then played for Keystone Lacrosse Club in Philadelphia for three years and have a vague memory of playing against Joe Anderson and the Alexandria Lacrosse Club one weekend on the Mall in Washington, DC. I told Jan I was hanging up my cleats when we first moved to Guam, but after we moved to Virginia Beach, I played four more years in a summer lacrosse league before we returned to Guam.

Jan and I completed our Navy careers as Captains with back to back DC tours. I finished up on the staff of the Assistant Secretary of the Navy, Installations and Environment and Jan as Chief Nurse at the National Naval Medical Center, Bethesda, MD. We thoroughly enjoyed our time in the Navy and found it very rewarding. There is a terrific bond working with people with a shared and important purpose. The inscription on the Seabee Memorial at Arlington National Cemetery says "We build, we fight, for peace, with freedom". Freedom is what makes our nation great, and I'm proud to have served in the Navy for 27 years defending it.

I retired from the Navy in 2000 and Jan followed in 2001. We loved our neighborhood, our kid's schools, our parish (St. John Neumann in Reston) and nearby job opportunities, so we remained in Northern Virginia to start our second careers. I went to work for a government consulting firm and have been working for the same client, the National Nuclear Security Administration, for the last 19 years managing programs to recapitalize facilities and special equipment at nuclear labs and plants. The kids are all grown and productively employed. Two of them served for a while in the Navy, Patrick as an Intelligence Specialist in the Special Warfare community, and Colleen as a Reserve Navy Nurse. Katie carried on the lacrosse tradition and was captain and MVP of her high school's Virginia state champion team. All three blessed us with granddaughters in the last eight months. Two year old Sullivan is now outnumbered by sister Margaret and cousins Brooke and Cora.

I lived in Cavanaugh Hall my first three years at ND. As a freshman, I could look out my dorm window and see the sun glistening on Our Lady on top of the Dome. When I did go to Sacred Heart Basilica (not very frequently), it was always through the "God, Country, Notre Dame" entrance on the east side. ND is a special place, and it gave me more than I could have imagined when I laid out my four "must haves". It provided a foundation for intellectual, spiritual, and professional growth, and my experience with the lacrosse club/fraternity was an important element of that journey. I am very fortunate and grateful to have been part of the team.

Captains John and Jan Moran's Retirement Ceremony

Dan Hartnett '74

Dan Hartnett, from Aurora, IL, came to Notre Dame in 1970. Playing midfield, Dan scored his only goal against Purdue in '73. He earned his law degree and served with the Army as a JAG in Europe. Following his 4 year Army stint, Dan worked in the Justice Department prosecuting criminal tax trials. He is now in private practice.

Army JAG Served in Germany

This is probably a very different kind of lacrosse story.

By the middle of 1971, I was in some serious trouble. I had been able to enroll at Notre Dame in 1970 because the Army had given me a scholarship; the catch was a four-year active duty commitment after graduation. As readers of a certain age will well remember, there was a certain amount of risk in making that bargain at that time, and to complicate the equation from my side, I had set my sights on securing a discretionary deferral of entry onto active duty until after I got into and then finished law school. To put my chances of getting the deferral in the best light possible, I knew I had to succeed at the six-week summer camp at Fort Riley after junior year. And at a scrawny 5'9" (maybe) and 125 lbs. (!), and not especially athletic, Something Had To Be Done.

I'm not sure how I found my way to the lacrosse club; to Midwesterners of that era, lacrosse was as alien as cricket.

But there I was. To paraphrase that infamous Fred Astaire screen test summary ("Can't sing, can't act, balding, can dance a little"), the report on me would have read, "Can't pass, can't shoot, can run a little." But everyone – everyone – was endlessly kind, encouraging, witty and funny, from Rich O'Leary to the team leaders; from the best players to all the rest. So I stayed with it.

In time, I learned I could hang in there sprinting what were then innocently called Indian laps on the cinder track under the football stadium stands, or running the stairs up to the top row and down again. Over time, I made modest improvements in dexterity, but my fatal lacrosse flaw was never being able to see the field in motion and know, instantly, where everyone would be in the next second, or two, or five. Seeing my play probably hurt a lot of eyes. Yet Rich and all the players were always positive, always encouraging and always patient. That was something given, not earned. I'm certain Rich set that tone, but I'm also convinced that tone was set by the players from the club's get-go and percolated down through the years.

My original plan worked. At Fort Riley in the summer of 1973, my lacrosse fitness ensured that I had no problem with the physical fitness demands. After an additional three weeks at Airborne School at Fort Benning, for which I had volunteered, I earned jump wings. The deferral came too.

Four years later, I went on active duty as an Army JAG (Judge Advocate General), prosecuting and defending criminal cases before courts martial in Stuttgart. It was the most marvelous apprenticeship for the trial lawyer I became. Mix together a society populated by young people, up to their eyeballs in exceedingly dangerous devices, away in a foreign country, and there was bound to be a lot of excitement. The endless stream of cases ranged from the screamingly funny to the heartbreakingly horrendous. For three years, every single day delivered a new adventure.

The Infantry and Armor officers I worked with were tough, brave people with a reflexive disdain for what they called REMFs ("Rear Echelon Mother f**ers") like an Army JAG , but they were willing to give me 30 seconds to convince them that I wasn't completely clueless when it came to their work. My standing was vastly elevated when, fortified by all that lacrosse running, I could easily keep up with the Infantry officers in their battalion training runs. And the jump wings came in handy before the jury when I defended a soldier charged in a brawl at the airborne unit in Vicenza, Italy. Living up close with people genuinely motivated by duty, honor and the individual's responsibility to the group was a gift I still marvel at more than 40 years later. I tried to do a good job for the U.S. Army, but no matter how good a job I did, the U.S. Army gave me far more than I gave it.

By the customary standards, my lacrosse adventure was utterly underwhelming (though I can remember with crystal clarity every goal I scored – there was only one, against Purdue – it's in the book!) and for that reason I've always kept my thoughts about it to myself. But the time has come. The gift I was given first by the Notre Dame Lacrosse Club and then by the Army – 'show up, do the best you can, and you may be surprised at the result' – has served me well then and ever after.

"Honor your father and your mother" applies to parents, certainly, but it also demands that we respect others who've nurtured us in important ways. Thanks to Rich O'Leary, may God rest his soul, and all the players who encouraged someone who really wasn't very good, because you helped that someone understand the importance of persevering; and you helped that someone better understand the importance of competing and cooperating. Thank you for opening a door of growth for someone who in the middle of 1971 was pretty worried about what lay in store for him.

I regret there are so many "I"s in this essay. The story to be told here isn't about me, it's about people who were unselfish and generous and helpful to me, and lots of others, and how those kindnesses reverberated at other times and in other ways the givers could never have anticipated.

Dan Hartnett, JAG, Boeblingen GER '78

185

Dan Hartnett (#9), middle, second row 1974

Chapter 3

The Plastic Head Era '75-'80

With the exit from Vietnam, America entered a period without military conflict. But the Cold War was still on though détente led to economic treaties and an attempt to normalize relations with the Communist Bloc. There was conflict in a new hot spot, the Middle East best exemplified by the 444-day Iranian hostage crisis. Jimmy Carter's presidency spanned most of this time and was marked by not only the Iran drama and a Moscow Olympics boycott in 1980 but also the Camp David Accords and a resumption of relations with China.

The wooden lacrosse stick was a thing of the past. Photos from these years show that the hybrid plastic head stick had taken over. Bacharach Rasin, which had dominated the early days of lacrosse equipment had yielded market share to Brine and the upstart STX. But more important than stick technology was the enforcement of Title IX. Passed in 1972, this regulation required equality in men's and women's sports and when Notre Dame elevated Women's Volleyball to varsity status, the Irish lacrosse program came along with it. Club President Bob Curley was one of the key individuals in laying the groundwork for the transition to varsity status. The package that Curley put together emphasized the strong history of the program, the outstanding support of the lacrosse alumni and the high level of participation in lacrosse at Notre Dame.

Over the history of Notre Dame Club Lacrosse, the Irish compiled a record of 114 wins and 91 losses in 17 seasons. Many of those wins came against established varsity programs like Air Force and Ohio State.

First Varsity Team, 1981

Mark Connelly '78

Editor's Note: Mark Connelly was the only ND Lacrosse Vet killed in war time. John Corcoran, John Fatti and Len Niessen collaborated on this piece.

Lacrosse played an important role in Patricia (PJ) Kane's meeting of her future husband Mark Connelly. It was 1974 at the Freshman Orientation barbecue and PJ noticed two guys throwing a lacrosse ball back and forth. She had played high school lacrosse and in fact had her stick back in her dorm. She went back and got the stick which became an ice breaker with Mark Connelly and his classmate Mark Carberry. The relationship between PJ and Mark became stronger as PJ volunteered to be the scorekeeper for the men's team.

Mark Connelly had come to ND from Camillus, NY, a Syracuse suburb. He had been a lacrosse summer teammate of John Fatti '76, and both went on to play for the Irish team. As a middie, Mark accounted for four goals during his abbreviated career. John Fatti remembers, "I was captain of the club team as Mark played for the A team as a sophomore. Then, due to needing to really buckle down in his premed courses, he left the lacrosse team as a junior- a big loss to the Irish midfield!". Showing his offensive skill on the '75 spring trip, Mark joined teammates Steve Tarnow, Fedele Volpe, Tom McHugh and Rich Caron, each scoring two goals in a 13-7 win over the University of Miami.

Mark earned the nickname "Stork" because of his long skinny legs and the glasses he wore under his lacrosse helmet.

The 1975 team picture shows "The Stork" in the back row, left side. In front of Mark are Coach O'Leary and teammate Matthew Kane (no relation to PJ). In front of them is PJ, who along with Lisa Michels (manager / statistician) became the first women associated with ND lacrosse.

Following his graduation in January 1978 with a BS degree in biology, Mark's life went into overdrive and resembled a perfectly executed fast break on the lacrosse field. He immediately entered medical school on an Army scholarship and married PJ shortly after. The young couple started their family while navigating the rigors of med school. Mark received his MD from Georgetown in '82 and joined the Army as a Captain and completed his residency at Martin Army Hospital at Ft. Benning.

Neither Mark nor PJ came from families with military background. But they were quick to recognize value of building their life with people who prioritized service to their country. It was a remarkable discovery for a young family searching for a place to build their life. PJ saw the beneficial influence it had on Mark and continues to see it flourish with her grown children.

Although it wasn't required for doctors, Mark completed jump school because he wanted "the full Army experience". He became a member of the family practice faculty at Ft. Benning. After leaving active duty in 1989, Mark accepted a position as associate director of the Department of Family and Community Medicine at Lancaster General Hospital.

Nikitas J. Zervanos, M.D., Mark's boss at Lancaster remembers Mark warmly. "He had a profound effect on our residency program. He was responsible for instituting morning report and daily devotions, and became a mentor to students, residents and faculty alike," Zervanos said. "You meet Mark, and you feel like he is already your friend. That's just the way it was with his neighbors, faculty, residents and students. Foremost, he was devoted to his wife PJ and his children, Meggan and Peter. He exemplified the concept of servant leader. I felt strongly that when the time came, and I would retire, he would take over the residency program. He had the gift of bringing out the best in the other person. One example of this was in his mentoring style. Mark could evaluate a resident and point out mistakes, but do it in such a way that he could make the resident feel good about it."

Because he had loved his time in the military, Mark chose to stay in the active reserves. Less than two years into his time at Lancaster, Mark was called back to active duty in December 1990 for Operation Desert Storm.

Dr. Zervanos recalls, "Before leaving to 'go off to war,' he came to my office to say goodbye, and for some reason, I wondered if he was telling me that he may not come back."

A member of the 142nd Medical Clearing Company, Major Connelly died on February 28, 1991, the last day of the 100 day Gulf War, when a land mine exploded as he was riding in a convoy from Kuwait City back to Saudi Arabia during Operation Desert Storm.

Mark Connelly was survived by his wife, PJ and their children Meggan and Peter who both followed their father into careers in medicine. Meggan is a physician's assistant, married to a Medicine and Pediatrics doctor, and Peter K. Connelly MD is an assistant professor at Froedtert / Medical College of Wisconsin. PJ described Mark, "He was full of positive energy and always sharing his love with family or friends."

After Mark's passing, PJ continued to live in the Lancaster area where she raised their children. She stayed for 17 years because it was the perfect environment for her family. PJ Kane Duling is a living example of how to continue living a purposeful life after dealing with catastrophic loss. Today, PJ embraces all opportunities to share Mark's memory with their fully grown children. PJ is a ***remarkable alumna*** of the ND lacrosse club and ND class of 1978.

The Mark A. Connelly Family Health Clinic at Ft. Gordon, Georgia has been named in Mark's honor.

The Lancaster General Hospital holds an annual medical education program for family physicians and to honor Mark they established the Mark A. Connelly Lecture as part of that program.

In 1991 Mark received Notre Dame's Corby Award posthumously, a recognition given to an alumnus who has distinguished himself in military service.

Mark touched many lives including his lacrosse teammates, his military brothers and sisters, his patients and his medical colleagues. As John Fatti sums up, "He was an amazing individual, teammate, colleague in the medical profession, soldier, and Christian."

Mark Connelly (back), Rich O'Leary,
Matthew Kane and PJ Kane Connelly

Mark Connelly (left), Jump School, 1987

Dr. Phil Volpe '77

Phil Volpe came to Notre Dame from Melville, Long Island, New York in 1973. He played attack on the Irish Club Lacrosse Team during his freshman year in the Spring of 1974. Phil graduated in 1977 with a BS in Preprofessional Studies and remained at ND in Grad School until 1979, when he departed for medical school. Upon graduation from the New York College of Osteopathic Medicine as valedictorian in 1983, Phil began a 30-year career as an Army Doctor. He served in numerous clinical, operational and leadership positions; deployed on multiple combat and humanitarian missions throughout the world with Army units and Joint Special Operations forces from all military branches. Phil culminated his military career in 2013 as the Commander of the Army Medical Department Center and School attaining the rank of Major General. Phil continues to serve as a professor in primary care, teaching military medicine to future military physicians at several medical schools. Phil was the 2007 ND Corby Award winner.

Long Island Attackman To Army Major General

While in high school in the early '70s, focused on athletics and unsure of my future path, I decided to follow my older brother's footsteps and attend the University of Notre Dame, to possibly become a dentist which was my brother's educational pursuit. After graduating from Walt Whitman High School in 1973 I headed to South Bend. Throughout high school I was on the football, wrestling and lacrosse teams. My primary sport was wrestling, I played lacrosse, as a hobby, to be with friends and as off-season conditioning for football and wrestling.

My brother, Fedele Volpe, played on the ND Lacrosse team (all four years) and he introduced me to some of the players and convinced me to come out and play. I joined the team my freshman year … essentially for the fun of it, as a break from studies, and for the challenges which athletics provides.

During that season, we came together as a very good team with a great bunch of guys who were very talented in both academics and athletics. We played our hearts out each and every game. One game that sticks out in my mind as especially rough was against Michigan State. Little did I know at the time how this experience would begin preparing me for a military career, where I would learn the term, *"suck it up and drive on, Soldier!"* We traveled up to MSU for an away game. Apparently, MSU had many of their varsity football players on their lacrosse team for off-season conditioning or to get credits in physical education. It was the roughest lacrosse game I ever experienced. They knocked the crap out of us, but we kept playing hard. I played a lot that game, scored a goal, but mostly remember that the bruises took some time to heal. We lost by one goal but we survived!

The Club Lacrosse team and players exemplified to me one of the big lessons in life that I share when speaking with today's youth: "whatever you chose to do, do it with passion!"

My ND lacrosse career did not last very long. I only played during my freshman year. While I enjoyed playing and being on the team, my focus switched to academics and becoming a physician.

After raising my grades, I was accepted at all 13 medical schools I had applied to, both MD & DO. So, in 1979, off I went to attend the New York College of Osteopathic

Medicine on Long Island just a 25-minute drive from my hometown.

I arrived at medical school in July of 1979 and began applying for various scholarship and loan programs. The military offered a Health Professions Scholarship Program (HPSP) which I applied for and was accepted by all three Services. I chose the Army program and thus, now being free from worry about paying for medical school, began my career in medicine, and unpredictably, as an Army Physician. Upon graduating as valedictorian in May 1983 with my Doctor of Osteopathic Medicine (DO) degree, I was commissioned onto active duty as an Army Captain (03) and sent off to Tripler Army Medical Center in Hawaii for specialty training in Family Medicine for three years. In 1986, upon becoming Licensed and Board Certified in Family Medicine, it was time to serve my four-year obligation.

My very first assignment was with the Multinational Forces and Observers (MFO) in Sinai, Egypt. MFO was a 13-nation peacekeeping force stationed along the border between Egypt and Israel, a result of the Camp David Accords of 1979 spearheaded by President Jimmy Carter, our ND Class of '77 graduation speaker. I was assigned as the Medical Officer In-Charge (OIC) of a multinational clinic at our north camp in El Gorah, Egypt. I discovered that the Army offers very similar aspects of teamwork, camaraderie, physical challenges and friendships that I enjoyed so much playing sports.

I drifted toward operational medicine, became proficient at it, and began teaching combat medics medical and trauma skills in the field environment.

I got to learn, see, and do "things" that a civilian physician would rarely, if ever, experience or be exposed to. In 1988 I was invited to "try out" for selection as a forward medical provider for the Joint Special Operations Command (JSOC) to augment elite special operations units. After being selected, I deployed on missions all over the world in support of our nation's best warriors. What a privilege to be given this huge and rare responsibility.

In December 1989, after making a combat parachute jump to support the 2nd Ranger Battalion on the airborne mission to seize Rio Hato Airfield during the invasion of Panama (Operation Just Cause), I was wounded by an enemy AK-47 round in my right hand while resuscitating an injured ranger on the airfield. After I stabilized him and cared for other casualties, a buddy wrapped my hand in bandages. But the wound became infected and took me out of action. Fortunately, our mission had been accomplished with securing that airfield and removing General Manuel Noriega (the dictator) from power. The military "grew" inside me with each passing operational experience.

I was honored to be selected as the Division Surgeon (senior physician) for the 82nd Airborne Division. Later I was selected as the Command Surgeon for the Joint Special Operations Command. I experienced the best leadership I had ever been exposed to during those two assignments and began asking myself, *"Can it possibly get better than this?"* Thus, thoughts about transitioning to that civilian practice which I had put on hold began to permeate my thinking. Then, one particular mission changed all that.

I felt that my final assignment would be as the command surgeon for JSOC … and that I had done all the exciting "stuff" one can do as a military physician who enjoyed "soldiering". Then, in 1993, I became the command surgeon and senior physician for Task Force Ranger which conducted the mission to arrest some "bad guys" in Mogadishu, Somalia. This came to be known as "The Battle of Mogadishu" … and was made famous by the book and movie entitled "Blackhawk Down."

That mission and the subsequent mass casualty situation exhausted every bit of my knowledge, energy and endurance. While our medical team performed heroically to save lives and treat dozens of seriously wounded warriors, we still lost 18 lives that day and suffered many casualties that required surgery in Somalia prior to evacuation out of Africa. The memories of that mission and the Battle of Mogadishu remain etched in my mind and in my heart forever. What I remember most vividly was the winning attitude, fighting spirit, selfless service and sacrifice of so many heroes that day. Task Force Ranger exemplified the phrases, *"never quit"*, *"never, never give up"*, and *"never leave a fallen comrade."* I was proud to be a part of it. I recognized that I was where I wanted to be, and how I wanted to spend the remainder of my career as a physician. I decided to remain an Army doctor and make the military my career by serving as long as I was permitted to; and to the best of my ability; and to always strive for ensuring our nation's warriors get the very best medical care our country can provide. They deserve it!

I went on serving in numerous staff and command positions at the executive levels up through a rank of Major General. I culminated an extremely rewarding career after 30 years on active duty in 2013. My final assignment was as the Commanding General of the Army Medical Department Center and School in San Antonio, Texas.

Since 2013, I have tried to utilize my experiences and what I had learned through the decades to develop the next generation of military physicians and military medical leaders. Currently, I teach at several medical schools as an Assistant Professor in primary care and military medicine. I also serve as a Special Government Employee (SGE), as a senior executive leadership mentor, in support of the Army Surgeon General. Additionally, I keep involved in several leader development ventures as a trainer, coach, mentor, and advisor. Some of the most enjoyable undertakings are those that provide an opportunity to share my experiences and the lessons learned along the way.

I will close with a quote from one of my magnificent mentors, "there is nothing like spending a career and a life doing honorable work with honorable people." That's what I got to experience! That's how I feel! And that is why I am truly blessed!

Go Irish!

Flying in back- Blackhawk at Korea DMZ, 2012

Task Force Ranger Surgeon, Mogadishu, Somalia, 1993

Visiting ND ROTC, 2008

Final Military Photo, 2013

Bob Speer '78

Bob Speer came to ND from Smithtown, NY. He played midfield on the lacrosse team and was a member of Army ROTC. Bob graduated from ND in 1978 with a BBA in Accounting and later earned an MBA from Indiana University. He retired as Colonel after a 28-year career having been Battalion Commander in the 82nd Airborne Division and Brigade Level Command of a Defense Agency operation. Bob served as a managing director at PricewaterhouseCoopers and also as Assistant Secretary of the Army under Presidents Obama and Trump

Vet Becomes Acting Secretary of the Army

My original connection to ND was through my mom and grandfather, both devout Catholics and avid fans of Notre Dame. In 1966, while living in Battle Creek, Michigan, we watched the game of the century, Notre Dame's 10-10 tie with Michigan State. I was locked in to be a life-long Irish fan!

As I chose a college, my Catholic roots and an enjoyment of ND football was just the beginning. Learning of the academic strengths and presence of ROTC at Notre Dame, I was won over from an alternative appointment to West Point.

Although family, common beliefs and opportunities guided me to ND, my personal attachment and commitment grew even stronger through participation in activities with fellow students, and as guided by the inspiration of the university's leadership.

Early at Notre Dame, I was encouraged to play lacrosse by fellow ROTC students and faculty, including Phil Volpe and Sandy Cochran. I never made it past the B – Team; yet I truly appreciated the camaraderie and developed a life-long love of playing sports. I actually enjoyed running the football stadium stairs, doing wind sprints, and practicing with a group of individuals united by pure enjoyment of sport. Unfortunately, my skills with a stick paled in comparison to my ability to run and enjoy a beer after a game. As such, I dropped lacrosse my sophomore year (still have my stick though) and stuck with ROTC, Bengal Bouts Boxing, and interhall football.

Nearly all of us cherish memories of our campus life with too many stories for this short essay. However, it was Father Ted's ROTC commissioning speech which provided an inspiration and enduring confidence in my direction. He read us a letter he had previously received from several evangelists, urging him to kick ROTC out of Notre Dame. They questioned; how a good Christian university could allow an instrument of the military on campus? Father Hesburgh read us his response, in which he said that while he did not condone war and prayed for its end, it had been part of human existence for millennia, as documented in the bible. As long as nations maintain a military, he said, ROTC would remain at Notre Dame, where it would build the strong character and moral ethics that our country needs in those who lead our military.

I found Father Hesburgh's words inspiring and an ever-present guide for my career in the profession of arms. It was a career with multiple deployments and operations. They included Desert Shield/Storm (ODS/DS) and Operation Iraqi Freedom (January 1991, while Deployed ODS/DS: XVIII Airborne Corps, watched the ND vs Colorado Orange Bowl in a tent via a rigged SATCOM feed in Northern Saudi Arabia, outside King Khalid Military City).

I had the opportunity to serve our country in many commands and alongside several high-profile leaders. Yet, it is those who I had the honor to serve alongside from day to day that left the most enduring mark.

I witnessed heroic actions during significant historical events, including in the Pentagon, when American Flight # 77 entered the building on 9-11-2001. Similar to scud missiles or mortar attacks in Saudi Arabia and Iraq, the human reactions and actions on 9-11 remain with me. Such memories drive me to continued service in recognition of those lost as do the routine daily memories of my brothers and sisters in arms.

One of my most cherished memories comes from an assignment to the 82d Airborne Division, where several Notre Dame graduates came together in significant leadership positions, including two former lacrosse players. Phil Volpe was the Division Surgeon – ND '77 (former Irish Lacrosse and retired as Major General); Emil Kovalchik, Battalion XO – ND '79 (retired Lieutenant Colonel); Mike Ramsey (Division Comptroller – ND '79 (retired Colonel and now Deputy Director of the Army budget; and myself,

Battalion Commander and Division Finance Officer – ND '78 (former Irish Lacrosse and retired Colonel).

All of these ND graduates are outstanding representatives of Notre Dame. I witnessed these leaders demonstrate strong character and sound moral ethics, much from the influence of their development and mentoring at Notre Dame (although Doctor Phil Volpe still had a wild-man side from his lacrosse days; making us do endless push-ups and sit-ups - nobody could hang with him).

Many are serving today and will in the future with a common bond beyond football or lacrosse. As the ND Lax Project allows us to reflect, we share values and life experiences of God, Country, Notre Dame.

My life's journey included a 28-year military career, successful business experiences, and a return to the federal government, where I had the privilege to serve as a Senate confirmed Presidential appointee for the Obama Administration and remained as the Acting Secretary of the Army during the transition to the Trump Administration. Or as some friends say, I was either "the Kiefer Sutherland - Designated Survivor" or "the Tim Allen - Last Man Standing" of the Obama Administration.

My business card has a familiar inscription; providing even greater insight to the foundation of the journey and the bonds that still last today: *God, Country, Notre Dame.*

LTC Bob Speer
82d Abn Div
Bn Command
ND 78
ND Lacrosse

Bob Speer '78 (back row, 2nd left), Phil Volpe '77 (back row, 4th from left)

207

Acting Secretary of the Army Bob Speer (r) (US Army Photo)

First Pitch- Nationals Park 2017

Joe Gromelski / Stars and Stripes

John Mandico '79

John Mandico came to ND from Northport, Long Island. A standout defenseman on the lacrosse team and Bengal Bout boxer, John graduated with a BS in Mathematics. During his Air Force career, he worked in computer security, was on the computer science faculty at the Air Force Academy, was Deputy Chief Information Officer at HQ USAF Space Command and served as social aide to President Ronald Reagan. While still in the Air Force, John worked as a Federal Account Exec at Hewlett Packard. After retiring from the USAF as a colonel, he coached high school lacrosse.

Defenseman Connects with The Gipper and Joe Montana

I was raised by a schoolteacher turned guidance counselor in Northport (Long Island), NY. He served in the Navy in during WWII. My father was a bright guy but quit high school in his junior year to enlist and "get into the fight". He did not talk much about his experience in the Pacific, however I came to learn later that he was a decent sailor but also a bit of a wise guy with the officers. He did not encourage me to pursue a military career. However, he did recommend I investigate Notre Dame when I started looking into colleges during my junior year of high school. I stumbled across ROTC when a buddy of mine went to talk to a guidance counselor about the US Air Force Academy. I went along for the ride but was not particularly interested in the discussion. I overheard the counselor tell my friend that it was too late to apply to an academy. However it was not too late to apply for an ROTC scholarship. I was still daydreaming when I heard the counselor say, "free tuition". Now he had my attention! As it turned out, I got accepted into ND, and was also thankfully awarded a 4-year Air Force ROTC scholarship. There was no other way I could have afforded ND.

I arrived at Notre Dame in late August 1975, a few days before most incoming freshmen. This was required by the Air Force ROTC detachment. Having grown up in an area with no military bases, I knew extraordinarily little about the military. My primary source of knowledge was from watching every episode of a TV show called, "Combat!" starring Vic Morrow as Sergeant Saunders. At my first drill period I got my uniform looking as "squared away" as possible, but when I reported to an upper classman in the ROTC parking lot, I marched right up and mistakenly saluted him with my left hand. He assumed, of course, that I was being a smart ass, and proceeded to loudly chew me out for the next couple of minutes. Welcome to the USAF.

I survived ROTC, and ND academics, primarily because of the bonds I formed with the lacrosse team. Being part of the team for four years was very meaningful and acted as a lifeline to me. I am not sure I would have made it through had it not been for the team.

I had been on a pilot-designated scholarship, and in my senior year I began flight instruction in a Cessna 141 at the South Bend Airport with a civilian instructor. I never felt that I was cut out for this. I was not doing well. My ROTC instructor,

Captain Gene Renuart (later 4-star General Renuart), intervened and tried to help me. But it was of no use; I simply could not manage the altitude sickness. My instructors concluded I was not a strong pilot candidate when I would get out of the cockpit after every flight, kneel, and kiss the ground.

As graduation neared, I was told I would be going into the "Comm" field, i.e., computers and communication systems. Hoping to get back to the East Coast (and the ocean) after graduation, I put in my request for Hanscom Air Force Base outside of Boston, and Langley Air Force Base in Virginia Beach. When Captain Renuart called me into to his office one spring afternoon and told me he had a surprise for me: I would get my wish of going to the East Coast, but not to the bases I requested. I was going to the Pentagon for my first assignment as a newly minted second Lieutenant.

I reported for my first day of active duty on September 15th, 1979. I had a terrific sponsor (a fellow Long Islander) who really helped me get settled into life as a junior officer at the Pentagon. I worked in a computer center, writing and maintaining programs for the defense budget. Halfway through my four-year tour I transitioned into a computer security job. I enjoyed life in Washington DC. During my four years there I earned my MBA by taking evening classes at the main campus of the University of Maryland in College Park. However, the highlight of my time in Washington was being selected as a White House Military Social Aide in 1980, serving President Ronald Reagan ("The Gipper") and First Lady Nancy Reagan. One of the highlights was the evening that I escorted Joe Montana and his wife at the State Dinner for Italy in 1981.

My next assignment was on the faculty of the Air Force Academy Computer Science Department. En route to Colorado Springs I spent 18 months as a full-time graduate student at Georgia Tech in Atlanta, earning my MS in Computer Science before reporting to the Academy. I arrived at USAFA in the summer of 1985. I had been there before, with the Notre Dame Lacrosse Team on our spring break trip during my junior year. It was on that trip that I got the idea of applying to teach and coach at USAFA. Seven years later, there I was. I coached the defense for two seasons but had to give it up due to the demands of being a university professor with no grad student teaching assistants (because it is strictly an undergraduate institution).

I resigned from active duty at the end of my four-year tour at the Academy. I transitioned to a position in the Air Force Reserve and continued my career as a part-time systems analyst at Peterson AFB in Colorado Springs. I also began a career with Hewlett Packard.

Aside from a two year full time tour of duty with the Air National Guard at Tyndall Air Force Base in Panama City, FL (while on leave-of-absence from HP), I spent the next ten years serving as a part-time reservist at various Air Force bases in Colorado. Then 9/11 happened.

I was recalled and activated to full-time status, but I was not deployed to the desert. I was assigned to a DoD computer and communications systems agency field office at Peterson

AFB, supporting HQ US Space Command. I was eventually assigned as the commander of the unit and was responsible for supporting the Director of Communications for the newly stood-up US Northern Command. I spent part of the summer of 2004 at a base in Bahrain, off the coast of Saudi Arabia. This was my only time in a combat zone.

I remained on active orders with the Air Force for ten years. My final tour of duty was at Air Force Space Command, where I wrote the 100-Day Plan for the stand-up of the Air Force's Cyber Warfare mission. In May 2010 I retired from the Air Force after 31 years of service at the rank of Colonel (O-6). I received an early retirement package from HP in 2007 while on military leave-of-absence.

For the next ten years I served as a high school lacrosse coach, the highlight of which was my two seasons as head coach at Air Academy High School, during which we went to the Colorado 4A state playoffs (semifinals in 2016, quarterfinals in 2017) and won the annual Sportsmanship Award in 2017, given to one high school per season by the state officials association.

John Mandico with The Gipper and Nancy Reagan

Dr. Peter Tan '79

Peter Tan came to Notre Dame from Washington DC. He majored in Pre-Professional Studies and graduated with a BS in 1979. In lacrosse, Pete played midfield. He served in the US Army, rising to the rank of colonel, while earning his DDS. He retired in 2018 after 36 years of active and reserve service

Peter Tan DDS Retires as US Army Colonel

When I arrived Notre Dame the Fall of 1975, I knew little about its history and mystique. I chose ND because of the reputation of its Pre-Professional Studies program for medical and dental schools. I had graduated from St. John's College High School, which was then a Christian Brothers, all-boys Army Junior ROTC college prep school in my hometown of Washington, D.C. St. Johns has a place in Notre Dame sports history primarily because it produced basketball star Collis Jones of the class of 1971 and football quarterback Coley O'Brien, whose heroics in the legendary 1966, 10-10 tie game with Michigan State and in the following week's 51-0 thrashing of USC were pivotal to that year's national championship.

I was truly a novice at lacrosse. And because Army ROTC and my course load left little time for anything else, I didn't participate in practice until my junior year. I played midfield. I remember that when I was running near the crease, I had a hard time with high speed passes, especially those that bounced off my helmet. There was a memorable practice on Cartier Field when I scored on the goalie, who then high-fived me because of the improbability of me scoring. But I was never told I shouldn't be there. And I enjoyed being with the guys, even though I wasn't up to their level. I was on the roster for my last two years, 1978 and 1979.

I left ND in May 1979 with a B.S. in Pre-Professional Studies and commissioned as a 2nd Lieutenant in the U.S. Army. I eventually married my wife Grace, whom I met when I was at ND and she was at Temple. She would be my rock of stability in the coming decades, for my career and for our three children and we will be celebrating our 38th anniversary this year.

After ND, I returned to DC and I graduated from the Howard University College of Dentistry. I was subsequently accepted into an oral and maxillofacial surgery residency at the University of Medicine-Dentistry of NJ and was accepted into a maxillofacial-craniofacial surgery and facial pain fellowship at St. Louis University School of Medicine. I also completed a dual Master of Science in Health Sciences degree in Public Health and Emergency/Disaster Management, graduated from the Command and General Staff College and the Air Force War College.

We traveled a long, varied, and rewarding road with the Army. I received my commission in the Field Artillery and after an educational delay for dental school, I began three years of active duty in a career that included 36 years of active and reserve service. I was fortunate to rise to the command level, where responsibilities were wide-ranging, continuous and 24/7. As the Reserve Commander for the Pacific Regional Dental Command, I was in charge of Hawaii, Korea, Japan, and the Pacific Island territories. Later, I was the Reserve Commander in Heidelberg Germany for the European Regional Dental Command. Subsequently, I was selected as the highest-ranking Dental Corps Reserve officer at the Office of The Surgeon General and the Pentagon, often acting as chair for Tri-Service, multi-specialty, and active duty working groups.

In 1990, during my Army duties, I established and then spent the next 30 years in private practice while also teaching part time as an Assistant Professor at the University of Maryland.

Grace and I are the proud parents of three and grandparents of four. Our eldest daughter Kristin is a pediatric intensive care nurse and the mother of two. Our son is now Dr./Captain Peter M. Tan, Jr., who is continuing the family tradition of serving in the Army Dental Corps as a maxillofacial surgeon and is the father of two sons. Finally, our son Ryan is attending West Virginia University on an ROTC scholarship and is a drilling Reservist, planning to commission and graduate in May 2021.

At the conclusion of my Army retirement ceremony in 2018, I recited the mottos of the institutions that shaped me. All were from the Army units I served: "No Fight, no Bite," "Excellence through Evaluation," "Centurions at the Ready," and "Army Strong." But I added one more in recognition of the importance of my ND experience—in the classroom, in the woods during Army training, and on the LAX field with my heavy wood lacrosse stick. That was, of course, "God, Country, Notre Dame."

Army Colonel Peter Tan (left), 2015

Mike Brogan '80

Mike Brogan came to ND from Orrville, Ohio in 1976. Playing midfield on the A team, Mike tallied 7 goals and 4 assists. Following NROTC, Mike rose to Brigadier General in the Marines and received the 2009 Corby Award at halftime of the ND-Navy game.

Most Improved Middie becomes Marine General

Each fall growing up in Orrville, Ohio—think Smucker's Jelly, Indiana basketball coach Bobby Knight and Notre Dame defensive line coach/defensive coordinator Joe Yonto—my family visited an aunt and uncle in Lucerne, Indiana, about two hours southwest of Notre Dame. Though certainly an occasion for my father to visit his sister, primarily the annual trip afforded my parents an opportunity to attend a Notre Dame football game with my aunt and uncle. The trips also planted in my mind the idea to attend Our Lady's University. Saturday afternoons listening to the Irish on the Mutual of Omaha Broadcasting Network and watching the Sunday morning highlight show, ". . . after an exchange of punts, Notre Dame takes over on the . . ." helped it grow. Fortunately, a Naval ROTC scholarship allowed me to realize my dream.

Before arriving at Notre Dame in August 1976, I had never seen a lacrosse game and knew almost nothing about the sport. (I suspect some teammates would suggest that even when I graduated in 1980, I still did not know much about the game.) I lived in Flanner Hall on the same floor/section as a second cousin, Tim "Woosh" Walsh '79. Timmy and one of his Flanner Hall suitemates, John "JV" Vercruysse '79, played lacrosse. Woosh grew up near Philadelphia and played lacrosse in high school. A crease attackman, Woosh had a great stick, but suffered from damaged wheels. JV, a native of the Detroit area, grew up playing hockey and easily transitioned those skills to become an accomplished defenseman.

Another of Timmy's suitemates, Mark "Jersey" Tallmadge '79, and I played interhall football in the fall of 1976. We watched several lacrosse games during that fall campaign. During one game, JV slid from his man to stop a fast break by burying his shoulder into the chest of the onrushing player, flipping the opponent over and jarring the ball loose. After seeing that hit, Jersey and I learned the rudiments to throw and catch a lacrosse ball, joined the club in the spring of '77 and played on the "B" Team. Jersey became a crease defenseman who loved to slide off picks and crush cutting attackmen or middies; I ran midfield.

A high school football and basketball player, I enjoyed the opportunity to hit people and found that the man-to-man, hardwood defense skills applied to the lacrosse field. Though not fast, I could run all game and with only minimal stick ability, I almost always took "man" during ground balls.

Junior and senior years, I played on the "A" Team. I managed one goal junior year and three senior year. During our Texas spring trip in my senior year, Rich awarded me the game ball after our victory at Texas A&M. That was the only game ball of my career and the only game in which I both scored a goal and had an assist. That season, my teammates awarded me the Most Improved Player trophy—my most cherished sports award.

Following graduation and commissioning in 1980 as a Marine second lieutenant, I completed The Basic School at Quantico, Virginia and Amphibious Assault Vehicle (AAV) Officer Course at Camp Pendleton, California before reporting to my first assignment at Marine Corps Air Station, Kaneohe Bay, Hawaii. At K-Bay I served as an AAV platoon commander leading 49 Marines and a Navy corpsman operating 12 amphibious tractors or amtracs. That time included a six-month deployment to the western Pacific aboard the USS Fresno (LST-1182). As a first lieutenant I worked as a maintenance management officer in an infantry battalion and made a second WESTPAC deployment.

After Hawaii, I served as a captain at Marine Barracks, Naval Weapons Station, Yorktown, Virginia, guarding nuclear weapons—though at the time, we could "neither confirm nor deny" the presence of nuclear weapons at the base. From there, I attended a year-long school at Quantico and then headed back to Camp Pendleton. Initially, I served in 3rd Assault Amphibian Battalion (3rd AABn) as an assistant logistics officer and then as an AAV company commander (245 Marines & Sailors), which included a deployment to Okinawa, Japan and service in Desert Shield and Desert Storm. Back at Camp Pendleton after the Gulf War, I spent three years as a major at the Amphibious Vehicle Test Branch as the logistics officer. While at AVTB, I completed work on a master's degree in business from Webster University.

Following another year of school at Quantico, I spent four years in a program office developing the next generation amphibious vehicle then returned to Camp Pendleton as a lieutenant colonel to command 3rd AABn (1465 Marines & Sailors). After two years in command, I attended a final year of school at Fort McNair in Washington, DC and received a second master's degree from National Defense University.

I then spent 20 months overseeing all Marine Corps infantry weapon, night vision equipment, non-lethal weapon, raids & reconnaissance and anti-tank weapon efforts before going back as a colonel to lead the advanced assault amphibious program office. After 30 months, the Marine Corps "frocked" me to brigadier general (the Corps allowed me to wear the star and use the title but continued to receive colonel's pay for eight months until I was promoted) and assigned me to command Marine Corps Systems Command (>2,500 Marines, Sailors and civil servants).

While at SYSCOM, the Undersecretary of Defense for Acquisition, Technology & Logistics assigned me the additional duty of Joint Program Executive Officer for the Mine Resistant Ambush Protected (MRAP) vehicle program. A truly rewarding effort, I oversaw the program that spent over $40 billion and delivered more than 20,000 lifesaving MRAPs. These armored, V-shaped hull trucks protected the occupants from the effects of improvised explosive devices (IEDs) in Iraq and Afghanistan. All the folks who worked on the MRAP program knew that we made a difference every day in the lives and limbs of Soldiers, Sailors, Airmen, Marines, Special Operators, Allies and Coalition Partners.

During this tour, the Notre Dame Alumni Association presented me the 2009 Reverend William Corby, CSC Award on the 50-yard line at halftime of the Navy game. Two teammates, Jersey and Bob "Harpo" Curley '80, attended the game with me and a short time later I received a letter from JV who also happened to go to the game.

In my final assignment, I served as the Commanding General of Marine Corps Training Command (>7,500 Marines, Sailors & civil servants). We provided occupational specialty training (military job-specific skills) to all Marines and Sailors who serve with Marines—both officer and enlisted—at 45 bases and stations across the country, most aboard sister service installations. I retired on 1 October 2011 after more than 31 years of active duty.

Notre Dame lacrosse gave a jock of all trades, master of none, the opportunity to compete at the intercollegiate level, build lasting memories and develop life-long friends. Who could ask for more?

Semper Fidelis, Mike

Captain Brogan (r), Desert Storm / Desert Shield 1990

224

AAV Splashing from Ft Hase Beach Headed to the USS Fresno, LST-1182 Nov '81

General Brogan (center) with Secretary of Defense, Ash Carter (left)

Blast Test of a Category II Cougar Mine Resistant Ambush Protected Vehicle, 2007

Figure 1Brigadier General Brogan Assumes Command of Marine Corps Systems Command Sept 2006

Bob Durgin '81

Long Islander Bob Durgin came to ND in 1977. He played midfield on the last teams of the club era and also the first of the varsity years. After graduation he earned a law degree and began a 21-year stint with the Marine Reserves, serving during Desert Storm and Operation Iraqi Freedom

---

The Story of the first goal in ND varsity History

I came to the University of Notre Dame in August of 1977 after playing one year of high school lacrosse under Walt Reese, coach of a very successful program at Copiague High School, a public high school in a blue-collar community on the south shore of Long Island in western Suffolk County.

I had first picked up a lacrosse stick that spring because most of the members of Coach Reese's Copiague Eagles football team also played lacrosse. I learned to play with a borrowed wooden stick with a red plastic head. After that first season of learning lacrosse, Coach Reese advised that it would "absolutely" be possible for me to play at Notre Dame as they were a club team and he suggested that I spend the summer honing my skills. Almost immediately, I ordered a new-fangled Brine lacrosse stick with a light aluminum shaft and plastic head. That stick (pictured here) would later score the first Notre Dame varsity goal against Radford University in March of 1981.

227

After spending much of the summer of 1977 using the new stick playing "wall ball" in Copiague, I arrived at Notre Dame and quickly found the lacrosse goals on Stepan Field. While practicing the under-hand shot perfected by Copiague's star players, two of the leaders of the Notre Dame club at the time, Pat Clynes and Tim Walsh, approached and invited me to join the club. So  began my journey as part of the tremendously close-knit lacrosse family within the larger Notre Dame family, led by our beloved coach, Rich O'Leary. I soon learned that this family would gather to renew the bonds of brotherhood for a lacrosse alumni weekend each fall.

The brothers I met during that journey remain remarkably close to this day. Over forty years later, many of us reunite for a long weekend of "Masters" lacrosse each January at the Florida Lacrosse Classic. Those weekends are filled with reminiscing about our shared misery practicing on the frozen ACC parking lots in the Februarys of South Bend winters, the road trips to places such as Denver and Colorado Springs (spring break 1978), Houston, Dallas and College Station (spring break 1980), or Lexington, Virginia and Baltimore (spring break 1981), as well as our individual and collective exploits on the lacrosse fields. There are frequent reminders of how I regularly announced it was, "Romp Time" in pregame sticks-up in 1981. We spend considerable time remembering our brothers who have departed us too early -- wonderful men like Rich, Nick Gehring, Tim Walsh, Pat Janks, Timmy Michels and Sean Corscadden. We truly are a brotherhood who love our time together and share a passion that still burns today for the amazing sport of lacrosse. In fact, the writing of this essay was interrupted by officiating lacrosse games in the suburbs of Charlotte, North Carolina this morning.

Although there are notable exceptions -- namely Brigadier General Mike Brogan and Colonel John Mandico – not many Notre Dame lacrosse players during the post-Vietnam years of 1977 to 1981 were bound for the military. My Marine Corps journey also started at Copiague High School, now named after Walter G. O'Connell, who had served as a Marine officer in World War II and lost his son, Daniel, also a Marine, in Vietnam. Then a guidance counselor, Mr. O'Connell initiated my Marine Corps journey by asking if I had interest in an ROTC. scholarship. Although that did not materialize, I learned of another Marine Corps program, the Platoon Leaders Class (PLC). The PLC program was particularly attractive as it had a "Law Option" which deferred active duty for those admitted to law school. After completing the PLC program during the summers of 1978 and 1980, admittance to Tulane University School of Law and graduating from Notre Dame, I was commissioned as a Marine Second Lieutenant.

Little did I anticipate that my PLC "option" would lead me to meet Susan, my beautiful bride of thirty-four years, transition from judge advocate to infantry and operations billets, deploy for Operations Desert Storm and Iraqi Freedom, and turn into a 21-year career in the Marine Corps Reserve retiring as a Lieutenant Colonel. After completing The Basic School and Naval Justice School, I was stationed at the Marine Corps Logistics Base, Barstow serving as a judge advocate and as aide-de-camp to Major General Hollis Davison. While in Barstow, Susan and I were married and our daughter, Amy, was born. We returned to New Orleans, where General Davison was then serving as Commanding General of the Fourth Marine Division, and I began my civilian career with the Montgomery, Barnett law firm.

During a social call on General and Mrs. Davison shortly thereafter, an impactful conversation went like this: "Captain Durgin, would you like a reserve billet? Yes, sir. Would you like a judge advocate billet? No, sir, I'm practicing law six days a week. I think there's a reserve infantry unit here in New Orleans." On the following Monday, I was asked to fill the billet of Executive Officer, Headquarters & Service Company, Third Battalion, 23rd Marines. Two years later, 3/23 was one of the first Marine reserve units activated in support of Operation Desert Storm, reporting on Thanksgiving weekend 1990, days before Amy's third birthday. We were fortunate to see only limited action before re-deploying in May 1991. While pursuing my legal, then business careers, I concurrently continued to serve in operations billets in the Marine Corps Reserve until retiring in 2004. My last deployment was to the Marine Corps Central Command Headquarters in Bahrain where I served as a

Senior Watch Officer in support of Operations Iraqi and Enduring Freedom.

I am extremely blessed to be a member of both the Notre Dame lacrosse and Marine Corps families. My Notre Dame lacrosse brothers have had a profound impact on my life and I will be forever thankful for the fatherly guidance Rich O'Leary provided. I am also blessed with a wonderful wife and three great children – Amy, Bryce (Notre Dame Class of 2011), and Trevor – and two beautiful granddaughters. When I think about myself as that young foster child attending Copiague High School I count the many blessings I have experienced by virtue of attending Notre Dame, developing life-long friendships with my lacrosse brothers, and serving in the Marine Corps, I can only ask, 'What though the odds?'

Thank you, Rich, Pat, Tim and every member of the Notre Dame lacrosse family!

Semper Fi

Bob Durgin, First (below) and Second (above) Gulf War

Appendix

Hats off to these other ND lacrosse veterans

Lieutenant Ed O'Gara '64, US Navy F8

"SATAN'S KITTENS" SCORE IN GUNNERY DEPLOYMENT – During a 2-week air-to-air gunnery deployment to NAF El Centro, California, the "Satan's Kittens" of VF-191 recorded 1,739 hits, including three century banners (100 hits each) and one double century banner (200 hits.)

Squadron pilots participating included (left to right in photo) Lieutenant Howie Nygard (Top Gun), Lieutenant Commanders Bob Geeding and Bill Asbell, Lieutenant Ed Ross, Lieutenants (j.g.) Steve Stevens, Billy Jo Craig, Jr. and Bill Bassett, Jr., Commander Ray Donnelly, Jr., commanding officer; Commander George Aitcheson, executive officer; Lieutenants Ed O'Gara, Chuck Lowry and Tom Letter, Lieutenants (j.g.) Terry Shaffer, Ed Wright and Jay Campbell, Lieutenant Commander Bill Turlay and Lieutenant Commander Mike Welch.

Lt Norm Findlay '66, US Navy (USS Navarro)

John Saur '65, US Air Force

John Brandau '67, US Army Reserves

Rich LaFrance '68, US Army

Phil Feola '68, US Army

Fred Morrison '68, US Navy

Lieutenant Billy "Spearfish" Foley '75, US Navy

Commander Bob Driscoll MD '77, US Navy

Lt Drew Daly '67, US Navy

Lt Fedele Volpe '75, US Navy

About the editors

Len Niessen graduated from Notre Dame with two degrees, an BA in Liberal Arts in 1968 and a BSEE in 1969. He worked in the computer industry for 48 years, first as a designer and later as a manager and program manager in server  development. He holds two patents in computer technology. Since retiring from Oracle Corporation in 2017, he and his wife Pat have spent the winter months in Naples, Florida. While at Notre Dame, Niessen played attack for the lacrosse team, getting a then-record 23 assists during the 1967 season. His career game came against Georgetown when he recorded 3 goals and 4 assists. Niessen is the author of "The Golden Years", a history of club lacrosse at Notre Dame as well as two novellas.

TD Paulius/Midwest Lacrosse Photography

Jerry Kammer graduated from Notre Dame in 1971 with a BA in Liberal Arts. He played goalie for the lacrosse team and was a co-captain his senior year. A Notre Dame connection led him to the Navajo Reservation in Arizona, where he was a teacher and coach at St. Michael School. His first newspaper job was with the Navajo Times. Kammer later became the Northern Mexico correspondent for the Arizona Republic, then a member of the paper's investigative team, and eventually its  Washington, D.C. correspondent. In 2003, he became the national immigration reporter for the San Diego Union Tribune. He

TD Paulius/Midwest Lacrosse Photography

received a Pulitzer in 2006 for helping to expose a bribery scandal centered on Rep. Randy "Duke" Cunningham of California. In 2009, Notre Dame awarded him the Rev. Robert Griffin, C.S.C., Award for achievement in writing. Last year he completed a book on immigration. It is titled *Losing Control: How a Left-Right Coalition Blocked Immigration Reform and Provoked the Backlash That Elected Trump.*

Dave Jurusik graduated from Notre Dame with a BA in Economics in 1973. He played midfield on the lacrosse team that won the Midwest Club Lacrosse Association championship in 1972 and served as co-captain with Rich Mullin when the team went 10-1 in 1973. Following graduation, Dave has worked for several national general contracting firms in the Metropolitan Washington Area. He's played club lacrosse with the HOUNDS and was a founding member of the Alexandria Lacrosse Club. He lives in suburban Washington, DC.

Rich O'Leary and Dave Jurusik

CPSIA information can be obtained
at www.ICGtesting.com
Printed in the USA
LVHW060953111121
703063LV00011B/104

9 781667 177892